Ian Wheeler – off to the World Cup.

From Weddings to World Cups

To Special friends.

Molly & Brian.

Love & best wishes.

Ian Wheater

From
WEDDINGS
to
WORLD CUPS

Memories of Fifty Years as a Journalist

Ian Wheeler

Librario

Published by
Librario Publishing Ltd.

ISBN : 978-1909238039

Copies can be ordered from retail
or via the internet at :

www.librario.com

or from :

Brough House
Milton Brodie
Kinloss
Morayshire
IV36 2UA

Tel / Fax : 01343 850178

Cover design and layout by Steven James
www.chimeracreations.co.uk

Printed and bound in the UK

To my wife Mildred, without whose support, help and encouragement the winding road through life, with its many ups and downs, would have been much, much less interesting and enjoyable.

Contents

Acknowledgements

Though the writer puts the actual words together he needs encouragement and backing from many people to translate those words into a book. In my case a huge 'thank you' goes to my wife Mildred and our extended family, especially daughter Laura (Morrison) whose business and computer skills made the book possible and Granddaughter Linzi Wheeler, son Graeme, brother Ronald, all of whom kept nudging me along with the writing. Outside the family I thank for their assistance in many ways; Sandy McGregor, LM Thomson, Dr Anette Cruickshank, Norman Watson, Mike Collins, David Carstairs, Eric Neish, Alan Thirde and Mark Lawson of Librario Publishing.

A special acknowledgement and thank you to DC Thomson & Co Ltd, Dundee for providing all the pictures from their extensive archives.

Introduction

It was not long after the start of the Second World War and the young lads were busy pulling at a loose sheet of corrugated iron on the north side of the local football ground, quaintly named Borough Brigs.

When they finally got it open enough they squeezed through, ran along the dip in the ground then climbed up and in among the big crowd watching the local team, Elgin City, play an armed forces Select.

The Select was one of many which played in this north-east of Scotland town during the war years, teams which featured players from leagues high above the level of the local team such as Frank Soo (Stoke City and England), Stan Mortensen (Blackpool and England), the already legendary Stan Matthews (Stoke City and England) and many, many more.

They showed in the control of the ball, the passing, the ability to score goals which, to a young lad, was all 'way above and beyond what he had seen before and which kindled in him a love of the game which lasted a life-time.

"I'll be in among them one day," he told his companions as they left the ground after the game – meaning as a player.

That didn't happen, hard though he tried in the lower reaches of the game . . . but he did get 'among the best' as a journalist and, more specifically, a sports writer.

The name Ian Wheeler is not bandied about as one of the great sports writers. He chose to work with a local newspaper, The Northern Scot in his native Elgin, then the D.C. Thomson organisation, neither of which, until the early 2000s, featured a writer's real name on the stories.

However, throughout what he calls, Football's Golden Years, he was known to just about every prominent manager and a huge number of players, from the ordinary to star names in club and international circles.

As he says himself, "What mattered wasn't who the writer was but that the stories helped sell papers and, of course, the people featured knew who had written them."

From his humble beginnings he reported stories from weddings, even one before it actually happened, funerals, local police and Sheriff Courts, Town and County Council meetings and the fascinating people involved. However, football became more and more an integral part of his working life.

It began in Scotland's north and north-east with games and players in the Highland League and grew and grew up 'through the ranks' of Scottish senior football in Dundee and Glasgow, to English senior football while based in Newcastle upon Tyne and Manchester. In international football with both Scotland and England, he covered four World Cup campaigns, one with England when thy won the World Cup and three with Scotland.

He was well known and accepted by the managerial greats like Alf Ramsey, Matt Busby and Bill and Bob Shankly as well as the stars on the pitch whom he had followed since their earliest days; Bobby Moore, George Best and Denis Law and the Charlton brothers to name but five!

Now, in retirement in the quiet of rural Fife, the memories – and the stories – come flooding back, of an era from the end of the second world war when even relatively small clubs had the opportunity of fame because the financial playing field was much more even than it is now. Players, whose salaries weren't all that bad if you played at a reasonable level, couldn't even dream of the ridiculous financial rewards 'on tap' today. British clubs were run by the local master butcher, baker or candlestick maker, not billionaire business men from countries with names hard to pronounce indulging in their whims.

If you lived in the times he recalls or if you don't know much about 'The Golden Years of Football' this is a read you will enjoy.

Chapter One

School Leaver to Cub Reporter

I had seen a typewriter, but never been close enough to learn anything about one. I had seen a telephone being used, but never used one.

A car? Something toffs had and not within range of ordinary mortals. I'd once had a drive in one for about a quarter-mile. The driver was a friend of my father's and I have never forgotten the make or number. An Austin, BLO 185, circa probably 1938 or thereabout. But that was it.

My story really started in what was an unreal time in just about every way. This was because we were three years into the Second World War, mid 1942 to be precise.

I was at school – and education was chaotic, with teachers going into the Services and others returning from retirement. I had no record of academic achievement – and still haven't though I had been a sports champion of my junior schools four times in succession. Yet all of a sudden I was being interviewed for a post as a reporter on the well-read local newspaper, still a month short of my fifteenth birthday.

It seems ridiculous in today's technically-driven, certificate-crazy world, but even more ridiculous will be the fact that I got the job and fifty years later retired from it, having worked in a large proportion of Scotland and England and travelled world-wide.

The explanation for my success in the interview had many facets. In the first place, the job had not been advertised. I had heard of a coming advertisement for the job of reporter from a neighbour, who worked on *The Northern Scot and Moray and Nairn Express* as it was then known and which was printed in my native Elgin in the county of Morayshire in north-east Scotland.

Not lacking in confidence, I decided not to write an application but, to go straight to the offices of the newspaper company and ask for an interview. They say being in the right place at the right time is the most important thing in life – and it was!

I made my request at the very moment the then editor, Stephen Young, Senior, was speaking to someone behind the counter. He was later to tell me that his immediate reaction was anger that someone was applying for a job that hadn't yet been advertised. There and then he asked me to follow him to his room one storey up. It didn't augur well when he first concentrated on trying to find out from where I had learned that a vacancy was to occur in the editorial department.

He later admitted that what impressed him was that I point-blank refused to reveal my source of information which, of course is a basic tenet of journalism, though I didn't know this at the time. So we went on from there into my background, my abilities, which I confess were few and my reason for wanting to interview and write.

I admitted that I honestly did not have a raging desire to be a reporter but I had once been told by an English teacher at the East End school, a Miss Kay, that my essays had the feel of a potential writer. I had found out enough about journalism in general to believe that I could cope with the work. It was also a fact that I was fed up about being at school and being messed about in the war-time chaos that passed for education.

When I left the *Northern Scot* for pastures new 11 years later, he confessed that my sheer cheek in getting in ahead of the advertisement – which never appeared, and my 'sharpness' as he called it, made him decide to give me a trial run, at 5/- a week (25p) which was 2/6 (12.5p) less than my friend from the same street who had started as an apprentice electrician.

So, at no great cost, I was off on a 50 year roller coaster of a ride as a reporter, sub-editor, assistant editor, sports writer, feature writer, sports editor and several posts in between. All based on the magnificent grounding I received with *The Northern Scot*!

We had an editorial department of an editor, Stephen Young, a sub-editor who was really a mix of editor, news editor, sub-editor and top level reporter in Miss Agnes Mary Robertson, a reporter, Mary Duncan and totally inexperienced me, with no shorthand, no typing ability and very little experience of meeting people. I was obviously more of a liability than an asset.

So, the first thing was to learn both basic skills.

On the shorthand front I took some lessons from a Pitman's expert. I didn't have time to finish the course, so my version all my working life was a sort of enlarged outlines, because I never got as far as abbreviations. However, over the years my style was readable by experts – as was proved when questions were asked about quotes alleged to be misquotes. The nightmare came in practice.

I have never been what you can call a religious person, too many questions, not enough answers, but to sharpen up my shorthand ability I attended morning service at St Giles Church in the middle of Elgin High Street most Sundays for a couple of years to note down the sermon from the Rev J M M Madill. Why? Because the editor alleged that he spoke at a steady pace.

What I didn't know was that after service every Sunday, Mr Madill handed over his sermon to the editor. But what the editor didn't know was that in mid-stride, so to speak, the Rev would alter his words in the passion of delivery. So, when I transcribed my notes they didn't match the original script. No matter how much I argued, the editor claimed I had got it wrong. It did nothing to endear me to him, I can assure you. When I went to the minister to get backing for my argument he also claimed he stuck strictly to his script. Not quite what you would expect from a servant of God!

There was also of course, the typewriter. The feather-fingered youth of today with their computers and soft touch keys don't have the foggiest about REAL typewriters. The one and only instrument was in the reporters' room, where Miss Robertson also had her desk, a smaller one at the window looking out over Elgin's High Street. The telephone 'exchange' linking various departments to the outside world sat on a bigger desk near the window.

The typewriter was an unforgiving beast, a large, heavy, dark presence waiting to hurt and humiliate in equal measure, an Underwood. It would have been better to have steel rods rather than fingers to depress the keys. To miss and slip in between those keys could mean a nasty abrasion and in my inexperience, I often missed! As with shorthand, I didn't have time to refine my typewriting skills and to this day, I am what is loosely described as a two finger typist – two on each hand that is.

Sometimes, the Underwood also had to be moved and I marvel to this day that no hernias were suffered in this daunting process. Yes, it was tough training on two fronts but, I and others survived, to our betterment, I believe.

Then came the momentous day when I was thrust out into the waiting world as a reporter! Well, it was momentous to me and I believed the world was waiting even though my pals mostly approached with "And how the hell did you get that job?" or "What kind of job is that?" which clearly indicated their level of appreciation. They mostly went on to further education and landed what my mother called 'grand jobs' or, did what my father, Charles Wheeler, had done many years previously and joined the town's biggest employer, Johnstone's Woollen Mill. Then known simply as 'the mill,' it is now famous world-wide as a maker of clothes for the discerning.

Not that the products in my father's day – he was engineer in charge of three huge looms – were in any way inferior but the ability to market them was in it infancy.

I always wondered if my father appreciated me being a reporter or whether he wanted me to get a 'proper job.' However, he did say frequently, "I'm glad you're not in the mill" so I suppose in that sense he was happy with my choice. While there was no precedent for journalism in the Wheeler family ancestry, he was a wonderful letter writer and an excellent speaker on Scotland's national poet, Robbie Burns. Maybe if he had got lucky like me at 14 . . . who knows!

Here I was though, out in the real world after a short spell, getting ready with as much shorthand as possible and fractional typing skills.

For years I preferred writing my stories in pencil, by hand, rather than using that infernal machine. I was learning the rudiments of producing a newspaper, sub-editing, laying out pages and supervising the compositors who, until you proved yourself, treated you like an annoyance.

Reporting was my designated path – and how eagerly I awaited my first real job. And it came, a report on a local wedding. Huge or what! Actually a form had been devised which you handed to the bride's family, they filled it in – names, occupations, church, flowers, reception and so on. When it was returned the reporter, in this instance me, wrote up a report. Not the world's most challenging journalistic test. Maybe it was an indication of my rising status, by this time another reporter had joined the fray. Cameron Bain, later to become deputy editor of the *Press and Journal* daily paper printed in Aberdeen.

But it wasn't all plain sailing. A couple of years down the line we had a form returned early. For some obscure reason it was written up and the wedding report appeared in the paper. Unfortunately that was a fortnight before the wedding actually happened. I hadn't done the report, yet I was sent down to cope with the very, very irate mother and her weeping daughter.

I did my best to explain the problem to a weeping mother and bride-to-be and left them, at least drying their eyes and promising not to take the matter further – in exchange for a report AFTER the event and a free wedding announcement advertisement.

I thought that was it – until that night. I was happily quick-stepping at the local dance when the bridegroom-to-be came in with his pals, fairly inebriated and laughing and joking about the wedding that still had to take place. Extricating myself reluctantly from the arms of my female partner, I edged my way to the cloakroom, picked up my coat and exited into the night with a sigh of relief because the same bridegroom-to-be was noted for his short temper and inclination to settle issues with his fists – and he was bigger and older than me. Cowardice on my part? I'd prefer to call it a planned strategic withdrawal.

My second job was at the opposite end of the scale – a death. If you were anything from well known to famous, a galley type was built up gradually as you did the things in life which made you either of those. Then, when you did 'go,' it was easy to rush through an obituary tribute.

In this case it was a relatively ordinary man who had made an impression in the pigeon racing world and was worth a mention in the news columns. I was off to a flyer (no pun intended) here in that I had kept pigeons and an uncle had a record as a successful pigeon racing enthusiast.

Unlike today's heartless approach to death, we were taught never to intrude on private grief. So it was a softly-softly contact with the surviving members of the family. The death notice would appear in the advertising columns. The reporting staff would make discreet inquiries as to who the deceased was and if he or she was interesting enough, would then gently approach the family on the lines of 'We have received the death notice of your husband/wife/father/mother and would, if you so wish, like to pay a small tribute to him/her in our news columns.'

About 99 per cent of the time it was 'all right, yes, come in' and you sat solemnly on the edge of a chair taking notes and pausing to let family tears flow while you did your best not to be affected, remembering all the time that you were, as the prevalent phrase has it, only doing your job.

I say 99 per cent because there were exceptions. Like the lady who opened the door dressed in all her finery and told the reporter to "bugger off". It hadn't been her who had put in the death notice and her husband had been a regular drunk who kept her short of money.

Looking at her clothes the reporter reckoned she must nevertheless have had a profitable sideline to be able to afford what she was wearing. Something which was confirmed in his mind the day after the funeral when she was cavorting at an expensive local dinner dance with a young male companion; one of several he saw her with over a period of time. Was it accidental that they were all, in the local parlance, 'well off?' Had she that many good friends who had a few bob and liked her company? I left others to judge.

Gradually I was gaining experience and the proof came when I was told to cover the police courts. They were held at 9.30 in the morning, Monday to Friday.

Mostly they were frequented by local section of low life that drank too much, swore too much or got involved in punch-ups. Nothing too serious because everyone knew to avoid these people, but they needed to be sorted with a fine or, occasionally, a few days in the local jail.

The population of Elgin at the time was about 8000 (it was hugely enhanced by servicemen and women, but that's another story) so everyone knew who you were or from which family you came.

Reporters, by the very nature of their job, were well known, so it was no surprise to be met after a case by the perpetrator of some minor misdemeanour, giving you the hard stare and the threat "that'd better no go in the paper." It often did of course, and either I looked tougher than I actually was or the Gods smiled on me because no threat was ever carried through – although, later in my journalistic career, it nearly was.

* * *

If, in all of this, you think that I was a young man obsessed by my new career and nothing else, you could not be further from the truth. Elgin was a wonderful place to grow up in for a teenager.

Yes, there was a war on and casualties from wounding, to prisoners of war, to death in action were frequent, but although I was close up on this in my work, you had to get on with life.

And what a life it was! We had in our midst, or were even outnumbered by soldiers and airmen, men and women. A huge Army camp on the eastern borders of Elgin at Pinefield, a huge RAF base at Lossiemouth, six miles to the north and 12 miles to the west, another huge RAF base at Kinloss.

I had taken dancing lessons from a matriarch of the ballroom variety, Miss Dunbar. We actually fell out over the way I wanted to dance and the strict rules by which she believed *I should*. But before the parting of those particular ways, I had learned to dance everything from the waltz to the quickstep and gradually added jive and jitterbug. Overall, a social attribute which was to stand me in excellent stead for the rest of my life.

We had dance halls like Elgin's Drill Hall, Lossiemouth Town Hall, Bishopmill Hall in Elgin's northern suburb, the Masonic Hall, just off the middle of town and other places not too far out of town. There were also the Assembly Rooms in Elgin, but that was far more expensive and posh events, which I didn't sample until after the war – and that on a Press ticket guaranteeing a report in the paper and maybe even a picture or two of local worthies enjoying time off.

My pals and I were in the 15-17 age group, fit and feisty and able to have a few drinks. We started early in those days, unencumbered by drugs and other similar temptations, before heading for the nearest dance. We took the floor for every dance over a six-hours spell and were still able to get up in the morning and do a full days work.

Of course we knew almost all the local girls, but new into the equation came lovely ATS and WAAF (army and RAF) girls, not much older than ourselves and hailing from such exotic places(!) as London, Manchester, Birmingham, Glasgow, Edinburgh and points such as, in one case, Stow-on-the-Wold and another, Ashby-de-la-Zouch. I had to look up a tattered old map in the office to find where the last two and others were!

Add to this delicious cocktail RAF Lossiemouth and Royal Engineers, Elgin, dance bands full of professional musicians from all over the country and it was a dancing heaven. It could have been a depressing time, wartime casualties, a black-out which prevented anyone showing a glimmer of light out of windows or doors. The few vehicles which were around having to cover headlamps so that only three small slits of light shone through. There was also food rationing, an almost non-existence of decent clothes to wear and fuel rationing among other depressants, but we survived all that and enjoyed life to the maximum possible.

The service girls were mostly away from home for the first time and revelled in their freedom. The 'opposition' for the local lads like myself involved in the dating game was a huge number of servicemen, but the girls were, fortunately, not uninterested in us.

I don't know how much they learned from us, but we certainly learned a lot from them. It was the days when girls were scared of getting pregnant out of wedlock – but that didn't stop the mutual interest in the leading up work! All you hear about nowadays is that the 1960s brought on the sexual revolution. That's from those not around in the 1940s! A whole lot of life was deadly serious, but conversely that meant having fun was enjoyed more intensely.

I actually had my first drink of beer at 15. A pal and I cycled the three miles to RAF Milltown for a dance organised by the WAAF. There was a bar on the side of the hall and no questions were asked when I requested a beer which cost, by memory, about 3d (just over 1p). I had one more later, so being that this was my first experience of alcohol, the ride back was a bit unsteady. I had met a charming young WAAF who was to help me into an advance in my kissing technique and improve on my fumbling attempts in other directions.

I danced with girls from all over Britain and worked out that the best outsiders were from Glasgow and Liverpool, though in the jive / jitterbug area, Brigitte from Edinburgh and 'Bubbles' the classic dizzy blonde (from London) topped the lot. On a Saturday night, in the smoke and sweat of a packed Masonic Hall (eighty couples and no latecomers) they soon created room for themselves and wore out a succession of partners with their sheer energy on the dance floor.

Since, as I said, girls in the 1940s didn't want to get pregnant except in marriage and condoms were whispered about, not openly on sale as they are today, things weren't easy for the extra amorous. Suppliers of condoms fell into three categories – local chemist shops, at least one men's barber and a little man called Johnny. Johnny constantly wore a soft hat, a raincoat about three sizes too large and long for him and walked about the centre of town with a brown suitcase which contained the 'merchandise'.

So the purchasing choices were going into a chemist's shop where everyone knew you and, probably a former female school acquaintance was serving, then asking specifically, and hoping you weren't blushing, to speak to the male assistant. Making your request in the barbers – full of men who knew you and your folks and who wore knowing smiles; or dealing with the wee man quickly and quietly just off the main street.

In the case of the latter you also had to deal with the accusation that his product wasn't guaranteed to be safe. Rumours abounded of unexpected pregnancies following the use of his wares, though I must confess I never came across any actual proof of this. Perhaps it was his 'competition' spreading false stories!

If you had nerves of steel and no worries about the comments, the chemist was undoubtedly the safest bet because of those rumours that the quality of Johnny's merchandise was suspect, even though enticingly cheaper. But imagine being well known and of a previously good character and seeing the glint in the girl's eye when you asked for the male assistant and she knew exactly why! Your life was guaranteed to take a downward turn as she told her friends what you had been up to and they told their friends who, in turn, were even more liberal with the news. Embarrassing moments for the buyer increased in direct ratio to the number of people who knew.

A friend of mine had a plus. He was approached by an extremely attractive girl who had previously ignored him and complimented on his nerve. There ensued a very intimate and pleasant association which lasted for over a year. Me? Let's say I never had any complaints or claims levelled against me.

* * *

Having digressed from my working life for a spell, let me round off the digression by recalling an issue which became a cornerstone of my future working life.

My first real recollection is of being four years old and being taken by my grandfather to the top of the wonderful Cooper Park at the foot of the street where I was born, Collie Street, by-named Shuttle Raw (Row) because so many people from the Mill lived there. He died not long afterwards, but I recall a small man, a dark suit, a walking stick, a cheery face with a heavy moustache topped off by a large, old fashioned cap. And he had with him a ball. He couldn't have been too nimble, but we kicked that ball back and forward until I was exhausted.

That began a love affair with football which is still there to this day. It led, when I was a teenager to joining a football team; meeting in a dingy little shop near the top of Elgin High Street owned by a cobbler who was our manager. The name was Willie Robertson. Small, pipe-smoking, plump, with a Glasgow-Lanarkshire type accent, we never knew his real background because all he would talk about was football.

I later realised that because he was on his own and dealt with a bunch of young lads, our parents were nervous of his attentions to us, but they needn't have worried. Both he and us lived and breathed football. He was also way ahead of his time. I was later to become close to such as Jock Stein, Scot Symon, Alf Ramsey, Bill Shankly, Matt Busby, Don Revie and other managerial 'greats' and 20-30 years before them he was preaching similar values to theirs if we wanted success at our level. He had also a tactical awareness not common then.

Though two full backs, three midfield players and five forwards was the usual formation at that time, he had us playing three or four at the back when the occasion demanded, or the centre-forward lying deep leaving the opposition centre-half puzzled as to whom to mark. I recall one particular spell where I was encouraged to forage forward from right back. You see it all the time now, but then it was unique. He pointed out that instead of simply marking the opposition I should take the ball to them.

His reasoning? Wingers at the time looked on their job as attacking the full back, for the full back to attack them was totally confusing. As Willie said "They don't know how to tackle so you'll either pass them and get in a cross, or be fouled and win a free kick." It worked like a dream and Willie Robertson's juveniles, as we were known, became a team which had success.

I am forever grateful to the two men who set me on the road in football and my parents, who encouraged that interest.

Chapter Two

A War Time Shock

I was steadily settling into my work. Wartime restrictions on information and lack of paper meant we couldn't report on many stories and didn't have room to enlarge even on the best of them. We knew of crashes involving aircraft which we couldn't report. The death of many soldiers at a pre-D-Day landing trial run in the Moray Firth was hushed up with dire warnings of what would happen if we so much as printed a whisper. But there were stories.

These were first reported in lists issued by the War Office – AFTER next of kin had been informed. I never liked going to the houses of casualties, but it had to be done and, even at 16, or 17 years of age I had developed a technique which didn't seem to upset families, most of whom I knew.

So, on this particular day – a grey one, rainy and cold, I set off to my own east end of Elgin to speak to a woman whose brother had been killed in action in Africa. I always wore a suit under a dark coat and a collar and tie and seconds after I had adjusted the tie and knocked on the door she answered.

"Hello Ian" she said, "What brings you here?"

I had a fleeting moment of surprise that she should be so cheery before saying "Actually it's about your brother, George."

A second later she went pure white and collapsed in a dead faint. I was a teenager with no knowledge whatever of what to do when ladies collapsed. I knelt down without the faintest idea of what to do next – and was only saved by the appearance of a near neighbour. She quickly settled the sister in a more comfortable position then, accusingly, said to me "What do you think you are doing coming here and doing this?"

I assembled my chaotic thoughts and was able to blurt out that I had come from the *Northern Scot* where we had received notice of the death, among others, of her brother. At which point the sister 'came round'. As she recovered we moved into the living room and there the terrible truth came out. She had not heard of their brother's death until I told her! It caused a huge row, because similar scenarios, even including the fainting, had happened nationwide. The result of yet another War Office botch-up. The casualty lists had gone out to newspapers BEFORE the next-of-kin had been informed. New rules were rushed into place and to my knowledge, the situation never happened again.

Elgin, as you will see if you study a map, is at the north end of the area where most of the world's Scotch whisky is produced. All the way up through Rothes, Craigellachie, Aberlour and so on there are distilleries pouring out gallon upon gallon of the golden brew. Naturally, there are people who try to appropriate some for their own use without financial expenditure.

One such appeared in court charged with an ingenious scheme involving tapping into a pipe which carried the whisky to a container. He was duly punished with a heavy fine and loss of the job he had in the distillery industry. I was discussing this with a very highly thought of member of Speyside society, a man who spent much on good causes in the area and who had achieved the status of being looked up to by most. He had however, the flaw of liking to boast about what he did.

I wasn't criticising the fellow in court, in fact I rated him a bit unlucky to have been caught to be honest.

"It's stupid to be caught," he said.

Sensing I was onto something I asked "So how do you know?"

We went for a walk and into a dingy building. From a recess in the back he took out what looked like the chest and back piece of a suit of armour. As I studied it, I tapped it with my knuckles and said, "It's hollow – and there's a wee tap kind of thing around the shoulder."

Off came his jacket, on went the 'armour' and on again the jacket. Certainly he looked a fraction more tubby, but that was it. It transpired he had friends who worked in several distilleries and who had access to the whisky being created. In his capacity as a well known and popular figure he visited these distilleries regularly. While there, the wee tap was opened and whisky poured in to the 'armour'. It held the equivalent of several bottles and after this was transferred to receptacles in a quiet, seemingly respectable house in a nearby town, it was divided up between those involved, which led to very happy and extremely cheap festive and celebratory occasions for those in collusion!

Another trick, explained by my Uncle Tom Wheeler who was a distillery cooper (cask maker) was to remove the top metal hoop holding the cask together, bore a small hole and extract a portion of the golden brew before plugging the hole and replacing the hoop. Tom claimed that though he knew about this trick he had never used it.

The courts were probably the places of most interest. To misquote an old *News of the World* claim, 'all human life was here.' I was fascinated by the deviousness and, more seriously, evil to which men and women could descend.

My parents and the great majority of folk I'd known as I grew up were decent and law abiding. But I quickly found out that there was a different type out there in the wider world infesting what should have been a simple and enjoyable life. I also found that a really 'good' court case became one of the top stories in newspapers every day or week.

Not that I was on the sidelines taking notes all the time. At 16-17 years of age I was becoming a reasonable reporter. The shorthand had got to the level where very few people could speak faster than I took notes. Fewer of my stories, when written, were torn up and consigned to the wastepaper basket by news editor Miss Robertson – it was her way of telling you to re-write in a way of which she approved.

So came the day I was sitting confidently in the Sheriff Court (the police court at 9.30 in the morning dealt with lesser cases, the Sheriff Court at 10.30 with more serious ones). As the Clerk to the Court read out the next case, which involved a man from a coastal village in the district, I realised it was one which nowadays is known as 'grooming' young girls for sexual pleasures (for the man that is). There was no way this would appear in my newspaper, *The Northern Scot*, but we were also freelance reporters for *The News of the World*, so I decided to stay on.

As the case unfolded there were details of how the accused, a cobbler, had gradually developed in three sisters a belief that they could give him sexual pleasure and break no laws. Suddenly Sheriff Hamilton Grierson, who was trying the case, leant forward to speak to the procurator fiscal, I couldn't hear what was being said and wondered why they were always looking over at me.

Also, in the Press box on that day were Press and Journal (Aberdeen) and Courant (Elgin) reporters, both a lot older than I was – but it was definitely me who was being studied. The case resumed and finally the man was found guilty and imprisoned. I was about to leave when I thought it would be better to delay a little and find out why I had been the subject of such interest. So I approached the Procurator as he was tidying his papers.

"What" I asked "was the reason for the sudden interest in me by the Sheriff?"

Without further ado came the answer, "He asked your age, I told him 16 or 17 as far as I knew and he replied that you are too young to be reporting on such cases, certainly in his court."

"But I'm only doing my job," I protested.

"I know that, you know that – and even he knows that," was the reply, "but he believes your tender ears should not be assaulted with stories of sexual deviation."

I got the picture, but continued to attend court and hear other such cases with nothing other than the odd glower from the Sheriff. I never did find out why the change in attitude but perhaps the Procurator, they were both members of the same club, had advised him to leave well alone and save some awkwardness.

* * *

One habit I had acquired at this time was smoking. I prided myself in being fit and trained regularly for football and cricket. However, one aspect of my job forced me into 'the fags'.

As well as *The Northern Scot*, the Moray and Nairn Newspaper Company had two other newspapers – *The Forres Gazette*, covering that area of Morayshire, and *The Strathspey Herald*, a Grantown based publication.

I never had much to do with *The Herald*, but on two days a week I would travel to Forres to cover stories in that area. The office was run by a lady who devoted her whole life to the company a Miss Bauchop (I never knew her first name). She filled many roles but was not a reporter although she knew everything that was going on in the town and 'guided' you towards stories fit for the paper.

To get to Forres I would board a bus in Elgin around eight in the morning and make the 12 mile journey. Nothing unusual in that? Then you obviously weren't around in the Second World War years! The bus was a creaking old affair with, it seemed, no springs or other forms of suspension. And to cap that, the seats consisted of thin wooden slats with gaps between each slat. There were blinds on all the bus windows and the driving and rear lights were partly covered because of the black-out during the long winter months, so apart from the internal discomfort, it was a gamble driving along a route which had bends and dips, no white centre lines, while trying to keep to a timetable. To this day I don't know how the drivers managed it but, better late than never, I go on record as saying they had my unstinting admiration.

"So what has that to do with smoking?" you ask. well . . .

It seemed everyone on that bus smoked and it was always full, with some passengers standing, so you are talking about 30 plus people. Gradually I came to the conclusion that if I couldn't beat them I would have to join them as I coughed and spluttered for the 30-40 minute journey; so I took the great leap into the unknown and started with the cheapest (and probably most lung-assaulting) packs of Woodbine.

When I think back in these days of smoking bans all over the place I reckon that anyone suggesting such a thing then would have been totally ignored and if he or she had persisted, been subjected to physical violence. Almost ALL men smoked, women and girls smoked, though less openly perhaps. So who was I to start a revolution?

It took me nearly 40 years to kick the habit – and I made it after a serious bout of flu. For ten days I couldn't look at a cigarette. On the eleventh I woke and felt the urge to start again.

"You've managed to have a break from smoking, so why not just leave cigarettes out permanently?" said my wife Mildred.

I grumbled and grunted for a few days, but somehow or other I managed and if you want to know how difficult that was, I had 'graduated' to 50, yes 50, cigarettes a day. Now of course, I am one of those 'I gave it up' bores, who keep advising people that smoking is bad for you!

I was now into my fourth year as a reporter, pretty confident of my ability and able to cover any story on which I was sent out. But I was also now facing being called up to the Armed Services. Unless you were in a reserved occupation, work so important to the national cause that you couldn't be allowed to leave it, you were heading for the Army, Navy or Air Force.

I knew of one reporter who argued that his work was essential and who was never called up, but I decided that, apart from anything else, the Services would be an interesting change and broaden my experience.

So, when my papers came telling me to report for a medical examination in Inverness, I was ready and willing. Inverness was, roughly 35 miles from Elgin. Nowadays by car, it is easily accessible. But this was 1945 and there was still a war on, transport was uncertain, to say the least. So, treble my journey to Forres. It was at best, uncomfortable but I made it by train, along with a few lads of the same age from Morayshire.

We were to miss actually serving in the war because it ended between the time of our medical and the surrender of Japan. We were still wanted though, because the future was uncertain and a previous war to end all wars had failed to do that, so no-one was sure what lay ahead. There were also replacements needed for many of the men and women who had done their stint in the war zones and other places.

So it was into a cold, inhospitable hall in Inverness to find out if we were fit enough for the Forces. Stripped down to our underpants I was next to a lad from the country and he was huge. My 5ft 7ins was dwarfed by his 6ft 3ins; he was about as broad as I was tall and had muscles where I'd never known they existed.

But the real revelation came when we had to be checked for a hernia or other problems in the nether regions. It was impossible not to glance down at other blokes, *er*, male equipment. Now I was not unused to being in the company of other youths and men when they were wearing nothing – after all I had played in football teams, since I was well short of my teens. You had to change from day clothes to football strips and back again before and after matches, either in the open or in a cold, damp and draughty hut (no luxury dressing rooms then). But I had never seen a development (?) on this scale. He was, indeed a big man, though a teenager in years.

Even though I had contracted bronchitis as a youngster and I had a bout of it regularly, I passed, as they said A1. I still think the authorities dropped their standards for us because of the number of very unfit looking lads who also made it. However, we passed and waited on our call-up papers. The perfect physical specimen? I later found out that he failed. Why? He had a previously unnoticed heart problem. As they say, never judge a book by its cover . . . or, a man by his . . . well, you know what I mean!

Chapter Three

You're in the
Forces Now

As a journalist I assumed the authorities would put me in a job involving writing of some sort but, true to form, they didn't. They chose the Fleet Air Arm, as an air mechanic. To tell the truth, I wasn't disappointed. I looked on it as a break, during which I could assess my future. I had little doubt that I would return to reporting when I was demobilised because I really had taken to the work.

It was September 1945, a few weeks after my birthday, when the summons came. I was told to report to Skegness, which I'd never heard of, to start my career (?) as a member of the Fleet Air Arm, known then as the Royal Naval Air Service.

At Elgin Station, then featuring a proud building, beautiful wooden floors and a station master who looked like one, not the whistle stop it is now, my whole family turned out. The weather was miserable, they were miserable and I wasn't all that bright and breezy myself.

Among them was my Uncle, Louie Shand, a former regular soldier who had seen service in many of the hot spots of the First World War, plus Afghanistan, what is now the Middle East and other places where the great British Commonwealth of Nations sent troops. He had the medals to prove it, though like so many who had seen real action, he seldom displayed them. His snippets of advice about mixing with people from all over the country and looking after myself were invaluable, during the two-plus years that followed.

When I finally got on board the train it was strange mixture of relief and anxiety. In Aberdeen I joined the London train heading for a change at Boston in Lincolnshire and then to Skegness. It was an incident-free journey, though another lad heading for the same destination joined the train at Dundee. His name was Alex Fleming and apart from the first few days after reporting in, I didn't see him again until 50 years later, crossing a street in Dundee, where I was by this time working for the second time. I'd like to have chatted, but I was in a car and in a line of moving traffic and couldn't stop.

So it was Skegness and the start of a military carer which was to be totally unnoticed by the authorities, unless they shook their collective heads over how often I got myself into minor trouble! But first it was the most vital thing in any serviceman's life – a number. Mine was LFX 773980. I came to know it meant Lee on Solent Forecastle (or, as the navy had it Fo'csle) division, number 773980, but why has always escaped me. Was I the 77-etc member of the Fleet Air Arm or something else? I never knew, but like everyone who has ever been in the Forces, I never forgot those letters and that number. I never used it, either, when I returned to Civvy Street, but it is imbedded in my memory like no other means of identification. Don't ask me those new-fangled PIN numbers, but I will easily go back 60 years and give you LFX 773980.

In my first few weeks in the service I made three mistakes. The first was to argue that a meal I was given – a bone with a bit of meat hanging apologetically on to it – was not a meal any normal person would accept; the second was to point out that white front (T-shirt) with which I was issued as part of my uniform was far too big for me and the third . . .

After being punished for the complaints about the food and the white front, by jogging round the drill square with a pack on my back, I went for a stroll and came across a bloke sitting by the side of a small pond with a fishing rod. He fiddled with a hook, stuck on some kind of bait and cast it out into the water. I had fished since I was five years old for trout, sea trout and salmon, so I had to ask what was happening.

"I'm fishing," was the reply – accompanied by a look which inferred I was stupid.

"What for?" I asked, restraining myself from giving him a mouthful.

This time he said it. "Are you stupid or something? Perch and a carp are in here."

That did it; I wasn't taking that off anyone. "Wouldn't call that fishing" I said.

Rising to his full height of about 5ft 6ins he came back with, "Do you know who I am?"

Which is where I made my third mistake "A funny wee man who is fishing for rubbish," I whipped back, getting ready for a real row.

He bent down, pulled on a jacket and pointed to two stripes on his sleeve. "I am," he fumed, "a naval lieutenant in the force you have obviously just joined and you are on a charge."

Having come from a life which was all about asking questions and seeking answers, I was now in an organisation where, I suddenly came to realise, you accepted orders, queried nothing and kept, overall, a low profile. And the outcome? Funnily enough nothing!

It appeared that, as he had no obvious signs of being an officer when I first spoke to him, it would have been awkward if I had argued a case along those lines, and as I was en route in a few days to my disciplinary training (!) near Warrington it was best to let things go. And I never did see that wee man again. If I had I'd have taken him for some real fishing on Scotland's rivers or lochs, though, in my advanced years I do now appreciate the intensity with which tens of thousands of anglers go after what are called coarse fish.

Hardly had we got used to wearing the navy uniform than it was moving on again – to Irlam just outside Manchester, for training in various disciplines, marching, using and parading with rifles, being taught the workings of various armaments like Bren guns, Lewis guns and hand grenades. I thoroughly enjoyed this period in my life, having always had an interest in guns and marching, as befits someone who grew up in the immediate pre-war and wartime eras. I had, of course, done a bit of shooting with airguns and .22 rifles in my time in Elgin, mostly at rabbits for the pot at home. The politically-correct in today's twisted logic world would deem that a terrible upbringing, but, in fact, I never wanted to shoot anyone and learned a discipline associating with explosive substances.

But, back to Irlam and the Fleet Air Arm. It was a great posting. The delights of Manchester just down the road and marvellous dances in nearby Warrington.

The NAAFI club in Manchester was a regular haunt which finances allowed and there I put to good use the 'training' at jive I'd learned in Elgin. I actually won a couple of competitions with different partners there and when those in charge decided that was enough, I switched to playing drums for my fellow serviceman Bob Bellaby from Doncaster, who was a brilliant pianist. We won again – and were promptly banned from competing. So, we switched to a pub in Hulme, situated in a typical Coronation Street and very similar to the Rovers Return in the imperishable TV 'soap'. We played our hearts out for the regulars who definitely enjoyed our playing because there was a steady flow of free pints landing on the piano top.

It wasn't all fun, though. We had to learn discipline, marching, hard physical exercise, use of guns; I fired everything from a rifle to a Bren and Lewis gun and threw a few grenades, real live ones. Fortunately cricket had taught me to lob as well as throw, so I got the explosion to happen far enough away from myself and the instructor, ducking down behind a batch of sandbags.

Some weren't so lucky. In our group no one was injured, but several grenades landed a lot too near their starting point – much to the disgust and anger of said instructors who obviously, and rightly, reckoned being blown up by friendly fire was scant reward for their help in making real servicemen of us!

One of the more boring of our duties was being on guard, especially at night and with about a million to one chance of having to challenge anyone intent on dire deeds inside the camp. I say boring, but it did have its compensations in my case at least. On this particular occasion I was close to the Wrens' quarters when there was a report that a 'peeping Tom' was disturbing the girls. We searched for the alleged offender, but found nothing.

"Get back outside the main door of the hut just in case," I was ordered by the Petty Officer in charge of the guard that night.

I had hardly settled to my duties when a whisper of – believe it or not "Hello sailor," came from behind me. I turned, rifle at the ready for trouble and there, outlined against the interior light, was the figure of a young Wren in a dressing gown. As I prepared to ask what the problem was, the dressing gown was opened wide – and torchlight from another girl illuminated the first girl completely.

Now, I was not inexperienced but strip-tease was not a feature of my life up to this point, so I perhaps did not appreciate fully the excellent view. I absorbed enough of it, however, to make this one guard duty which I remember to this day. The perfect ending, of course, would have been to meet the young lady at, say a dance, when she was fully dressed and say the immortal line, "Hello there, I didn't recognise you with your clothes on." Sadly it never happened because, to be perfectly honest, I hadn't really seen her face!

Me and my mates did put our marching to good use on at least one occasion, when we took part in the Victory parade in Manchester which celebrated the winning of the Second World War. Though we felt a bit like imposters, not having actually served in a war zone, we did the appropriate marching – and this behind a pipe band, which gave me an excuse to tell my English mates how privileged they were!

Here, let me digress again . . .

I have told you about my passion for football and during my service time it was fully sated. I had seen top class players appearing in service select teams in and around Elgin – Joe Harvey, later to captain Newcastle United to FA Cup glory, Stan Mortensen and Stan Matthews, true greats of the game in England, amongst others. But now I was in my service time in the north-west Midlands and south of England, close up to some of the outstanding teams and individuals of their time.

I stood on the real Kop at Liverpool; saw Manchester United's bombed Old Trafford ground and the two teams from the area playing at Manchester City's Maine Road; watched a Derby County team with the magical forward trio of Raich Carter, Stamps and Peter Doherty run rings round the opposition, and was a regular at Portsmouth's Fratton Park when they had the Froggat brothers and the inimitable Jimmy Dickinson in the colours.

I was to get to know many of them in later years though I didn't realise that at the time. Among them a Preston North End winger and England 'great' Tom Finney and the wing-half behind him, Bill Shankly, plus the hard-working inside forward by the name of Bob Paisley. They DEFINITELY made an impact on the game in the years ahead!

* * *

Irlam behind me it was on to Hednesford, to learn how to be an air mechanic (airframes). First thing to impress about the new surroundings was that it was at the top of a hill, a steep hill, and we had to carry our gear, kitbag, hammock and tool-box, all the way to the top, The encouraging cries from attendant leading seamen and petty officers, as we square bashed, were couched in terms of blasphemy never quite matched even by their disciplinary brothers. It hadn't a lot to do with aeroplanes or our finer feelings, but it certainly got us up that hill.

The worst winter of my life was spent at Hednesford. The snow fell, the temperature rocketed downwards and I waited for a return of my annual winter bout of bronchitis to take me into a warm hospital ward, somewhere civilised. But even that let me down. For three years, in winter at home, I'd had to wear a thick under-vest and a sort of red flannel square covering my chest and a smear of ointment that was supposed to calm down the inflammation in my lungs.

"That'll keep the bronchitis at bay," I was told. It didn't, so I was then told that if I hadn't been cocooned it would have been a lot worse. So I was a certainty to suffer at Hednesford, because my chest 'armour' now consisted of a navy 'white front' a T-shirt type garment, white with a navy stripe round the collar, worn under the traditional navy jumper. This meant almost the whole of my chest was exposed to all weathers behind only a thin covering of cotton. We should have also had a swop for the white front, a thick blue jersey for winter wear, but for some reason never explained – the services never have to explain, don't y'know, our allocation didn't arrive until we were posted on to the sunny, warm south coast.

So I waited and hoped, stupidly, that I'd become ill. But it never happened. In fact it hasn't happened since, other than briefly when it could have been a chest cold. My conclusion? That though I would not recommend the procedure for sufferers from chest complaints it does make you wonder.

The training at Hednesford was thorough and even a non-mechanical person like me did learn how to look after the airframe, the body and wings, of an aeroplane. It was nothing as advanced as today's jet propelled affairs, but modern for those of the time. The discipline, in the sense of square bashing and the like, diminished to the point of no return, though we still had to adhere to the navy's rules about our conduct . . . and we did, to a degree!

Although a bit isolated, the camp was in the centre of an area where Cannock, Wolverhampton, Birmingham, Derby and other east and west Midland points were accessible by bus and train and there was always a chance of a lift in one of our lorries if it happened to be going for supplies of one kind and another.

The football grounds were a great attraction, as were dance halls and pubs; a group of us sampled them all on week-end leave or any other occasion possible. On one memorable pub crawl in Wolverhampton, where I learned to like English draught beer, three or four of us landed in the tram depot in the city searching for transport home.

"Sorry lads, the last one is gone," said the man who stoked the boilers, "but you're welcome to find a place for a kip."

And we did, on a heap of nutty slack (small coals). Wrapped in our great coats it wasn't too bad, especially as we had learned on crowded trains, the norm at the time, to grab a rest whenever and wherever possible, even on the luggage rack. First tram in the morning we were off, hurrying to get back to camp before roll call. We had nicked out through a well known hole in the fence surrounding the camp. If you timed the guards, this wasn't difficult as they used it themselves because they were drawn from our unit and we were heading back the same way. Pretty dishevelled and unshaven we were just inside our territory when a cheery voice rang out,

"Good morning lads, I see you are up and about early. Keeping fit, no doubt, enjoying the fresh morning air."

It was the camp padre and thinking back, it could have been worse – a guard or a petty officer looking for a few bodies to put on a charge and thereby enhancing his reputation as a hard man.

We mumbled our replies "Good morning . . . yes, nice day," and so on.

Still smiling benignly he replied, "So I will see you at service on Sunday, in fact EVERY Sunday, won't I"

It wasn't a request, it wasn't even an order because that wasn't his way, but let it be said that we attended church regularly for the rest of our stay. However, we made it for morning parade, unshaven, but hastily washed and looking reasonably keen and fresh.

While marching and square bashing in general were behind us, we still marched to classes, physical training, football practice and the like and on one of those marches a voice from a roadside trench being dug said "Hey Ian."

I looked down and there was Willie Carr. Willie was a tough as nails Glaswegian who had worked as a labourer in the Clyde shipyards. He could have claimed a reserved occupation, but decided to chance a spell in the Services. For no particular reason than we were fellow Scots, we palled about during disciplinary training. Came Christmas Eve 1945 and he persuaded me to join him at midnight mass in Manchester Cathedral. We'd had a few pints, I wouldn't normally have gone but, like any journalist, I was always open to new experiences. As he knelt in prayer, I could see he was crying. Tough as old boots but, shedding tears. I could hardly believe it.

"Come on," he said, halfway through the service and off we went – to Victoria railway station. A train for the north was leaving "I'm off", he said and slipped down into another train bay.

That was the last I saw of him until the meeting in Hednesford. He was serving a sentence for desertion, but I managed to persuade the padre that it would do no harm for me to have a chat with him and help make him realise not everyone was against him. So I got the full story. At

Mass he had suddenly turned really homesick. He had a wife and child and couldn't bear to spend Christmas away from them.

Somehow or other he had got on the train from the wrong side, with help from a couple of army lads going on official leave. Then he had avoided the ticket collector – again with help from other servicemen, actually managed to get on a Glasgow train at Preston, left it a couple of stops before Glasgow, hitched a lift and arrived home in time to have what was left of Christmas and a chunk of New Year with his own folk.

"They didn't catch me, I went into the polis station and gave myself up," he said. "Probably saved me from worse than a few months in the glass-house." The 'glass-house' was the top navy detention centre and feared by all of us. However, I don't think even that fazed Willie, he really was tough. To my regret I never got together with him again, although I did see him.

It was a Partick Thistle – Celtic football match at Thistle's Firhill. By this time I was a sports writer and covering the game for *The Sunday Post*. Usually, I waited and phoned my report from the ground. This time, though, and for no particular reason, I left with the crowd and as it swirled its way towards the town I saw a crop of red hair and below it the unforgettable Carr face. I shouted and waved as best I could and he spotted me. Next thing he'd disappeared in another crowd swirl and that was that. Maybe I should have found out where he lived and visited, but I didn't. I hope time has been kind to him – a hard man yes, but, to me, a real pal.

And one last and abiding memory of Hednesford is of a boxing event. In Elgin during my teens there was a boxing booth run by a promoter called Tommy Woods, part of a travelling fair which was 'frozen' where it was situated when war broke out. This canvas covered booth, with a ring inside and accommodation for about 100 paying customers drew an amazing number of high profile boxers who were perhaps past their best, but still formidable in their own environment. Ex Scottish flyweight champion Freddie Tennant, bantam weight champion Jim Brady, lightweight Tiny Bostock, welterweight Bill

Stevens were among them, not to mention Elgin lad Jock Riddell, a reasonable heavy weight.

Local lads were offered £1 if they could last three rounds with any of those booth-based fighters, I can't remember any who did. I didn't enter the ring as a competitor, even though I had boxed a wee bit, but as a reporter, I did occasional bits and pieces about the fighters. This way, I met especially Freddie Tennant who would take me into the ring and invite me to hit him. If I ever landed a decent punch on him I can't recall it. He was brilliant at avoiding blows and occasionally would direct a punch at me which, had it been full force would have landed me in hospital.

But, back to Hednesford. I'd trained with a few boxers in our unit and was told to report to the gym along with three others. When we did it was to see a man with a shock of black wavy hair and a yellow complexion working out in the ring. As a unit, the four of us went into the ring and were invited to try and land a few blows on the boxer. A bit nervously at first we tried, then as we warmed up, tried harder. Being that there were four of us, the odd punch did land, but mostly he blocked or dodged them and in return, did a Freddie Tennant by lightly tapping a glove on an exposed jaw or body.

After about ten minutes of this a halt was called and we were introduced. Our opponent was Freddie Mills, the same Mills who later became light-heavyweight champion of the world in the days when titles really meant something. And his yellow complexion? That resulted from a period with the RAF in Malaya and an enforced intake of a drug called mepachrine, which kept malaria at bay, but turned the user's skin yellow in the process.

The final big moment at Hednesford came when we were given the results of our exams on all aspects of our jobs-to-be. I'll be honest, I didn't expect to pass. I hoped perhaps to get a second go, but in fact, I qualified as an air mechanic (airframes) with high marks. Does that tell you about the course or, was I better than I thought? I don't know, but I didn't care much, either. I was through and off, I hoped, to a posting which had everything, a foreign land with plenty of sun, sea and anything else you can think on. In fact, when my turn came, I was told I WAS off to an island – Thorney Island, in fact.

Brilliant, but where was it? I couldn't spot it on the tattered map of the world which had the index pages missing, so I chanced a chat with a petty officer.

"A brilliant place," he said, dead pan. There's what you asked about, sea, sand and the rest, and it's warm for most of the year."

"Fine, but where is it?" I asked again.

He paused, grinned and said, "Hampshire, actually. On the south coast not far from Portsmouth." He didn't then fall about laughing, but he came close, underlining my reasoning that his kind was a sadistic lot. A home posting . . . again! My dreams fell apart, but the dye, as they say, was cast.

Our squadron number was 703 and we were a NASWDU an abbreviation for a naval air-sea warfare development unit. What that amounted to was loading our various aircraft, Mosquito's, Barracudas, Avengers, Seafires (the naval version of the Spitfire) with machine guns, cannon, bombs and/or torpedoes and such-like deadly armaments, then seeing the planes and pilots off to fire them one at a time, two at a time, then all at once.

If the plane stayed in the air and didn't get blown backwards that was the amount of hardware it could accommodate and everyone congratulated each other on success. There were rumours that one had actually ended up in the English Channel after unleashing all its firepower at once and being propelled backwards and downwards, but it was never confirmed.

As an airframe mechanic, apart from checking 'my' planes regularly; two Mosquito's and the commanding officer Lt Commander Dundas's Oxford, I had to carry out any needed alterations to the body and wings of the plane. This was mostly under supervision, because wisely, the Fleet Air Arm didn't fully trust our abilities to get things absolutely spot on. I didn't do too badly other than . . . I had to replace some fabric on the wing of a Mosquito. Once you did a job, you signed a book, known to us as the 'blood book,' and flew in the repaired plane. It certainly ensured you did a good job!

As I loved flying I eyed the land below and the sky above before switching my attention to my repair. At first everything looked fine. Then I noticed a slight ripple on the surface of the fabric. I'll soon sort that, I thought. Then the ripple got bigger . . . and bigger . . . until suddenly, the new fabric disappeared into space. Apart from a slight adjustment in trim, the pilot flew on and as planned, returned to base on time.

He could have had me in deep trouble but instead, asked a petty officer (the equivalent of a sergeant in the army) to look at things. I'm glad he did because it was found that the dope (the paint-type substance used to shrink and tighten up the fabric) was so old that it was next door to useless. I re-did the repair and there was no more trouble with it.

I also had a narrow escape with the commanding officer's Oxford. It had barely taken off, with him on board, when an engine cowling disappeared. It later transpired it landed in a field of cows and the farmer received compensation for the cows being unable to produce milk for several days. The plane returned to our airfield and I was summoned before the C.O. Though the nacelle was in two pieces round the engine it was my duty to see it was secure. I was certain it had been when I did my pre-flight checks but it seemed I was wrong.

Just as I was being lined up for a charge of neglect however, my engine fitter 'Lofty' Waring, from Leamington Spa, had remembered something and taken off the nacelle to inspect an engine part. Because of his honesty and my innocence of any neglect, the matter was dropped – except for a severe tongue lashing from the C.O.

* * *

My father had been a pipe band drummer with the Territorial Army in his young days, 1918 and into the 1920's. The enjoyment of drumming passed down to me – but more jazz band than pipes. I had a few goes with bands in Elgin and that stint while doing our training in Irlam and around. So when I heard the Thorney Island station jazz band needed a drummer, I was in like a flash. The band consisted, postings allowing, of a professional pianist, professional bass player, saxophonist, trumpeter and drummer. I earned a couple of pounds every time we played so, on top of my service pay £3.10 shillings a week, (10/- of which I sent home to my parents) it made me pretty well off and able to afford a regular few pints.

Nowadays there is always screaming hordes of girls ready, able and willing to have fun with pop stars. So what's new? OK the numbers weren't as big, but a band player was always an attraction for some of the ladies dancing out in front of us. I dated a few, the most regular being Ivy, who lived in Emsworth, the nearest village to the camp. When I had time between working, playing football and playing in the band, we'd attend the local dances and 'the pictures' at the local cinema.

Her mother couldn't stand Scotsmen, I never found out why, so any meeting at her home, where her father had a cobbler's business, was very infrequent. Through association though I came to meet her brother, John Vosey. He had been in the navy and was demobbed. His hobby was building a motor boat and in this I helped as a labourer.

Slowly, the boat took shape beside the mud flats that were flooded when the tide came in and in late 1946 she was ready for launching. No Royal presence, no champagne bottles, just the two of us somehow getting her into the water. John fired up the engine and we did a tour of the bay. Everything was fine and gradually we extended our trips, until we actually sailed round the Isle of Wight. We were getting too confident though and on one occasion, in the open Channel, the engine failed to start. A choppy sea and a running tide didn't help our confidence and we spent a worrying half-hour or so until John managed to re-start the engine. We didn't hang about and were berthed safely very soon after.

I made my excuses and managed to avoid any further trips. Flying I didn't mind, but despite a fishing boat ancestry on my mother's side, the sea has always been something I liked to look out or down on, not sail in.

It was a busy life, which because I had always been interested in aeroplanes, I mostly enjoyed. The drawbacks were a few pathetically snobbish officers and a bullying chief petty officer. With experience gained, we gradually learned to keep out of their way or give them no excuse to annoy us. I had one narrow escape though from the chief PO, called Sharman.

Men over 21 got a ration of a tot of rum every day. Some didn't drink their allocation and they would give we younger lads a share, called 'sippers'. Standing them the odd pint in the canteen later was a fair return. On average you would perhaps get one sip every few days, but on this occasion, because one of the older lads was having a birthday, the rum flowed freely. I can't remember how much I drank, but when I went to work on one of my planes, a Mosquito, I fell sound asleep in the cockpit. I was well under when my fitter Lofty Waring, shook me awake to warn of the appearance of the hated chief.

Have you ever wakened suddenly out of a drunken sleep? If so you'll understand how, in a daze, I shot up, climbed out of the cockpit and slid onto the wing. That should have had me standing beside the cockpit, alert and ready to get on with my work. However, I was wearing navy boots which were well worn, with the soles smooth and slippy. My boots lost their grip, I tobogganed down the wing, shot off the edge and hit a hangar side door, which was being repaired.

It was solid metal and heavy. As I had hit it low down, it toppled over on to me. My right leg took the force of the blow and to this day I have an indent on my thigh where the door landed. I must have passed out for a few seconds because next thing I knew was a few of my mates lifting the door off me and the chief PO, ordering them to lift me to the sick bay, where I spent a pleasant couple of days excused duty and treated like a person, not a number.

At Thorney we had a couple of helicopters. Though I didn't work on them, I knew about their operations. Fitted with floats instead of wheels, so that they could land on water, their main task was developing sonar buoys. These were red 'tubes' of what looked like cardboard which were dropped into the sea in a planned pattern. From them a sonic pinging sound reached down into the water. Should there be anything hiding under the surface the sonic 'ping' would shorten and give an outline of that object.

The pilots who flew the helicopters were specialists in their field and, of course, could hover above an object on land or sea – any object. The war having finished there wasn't much chance of an enemy submarine being out there in the English Channel, but the tests went on just in case. And the pilots found something to hover over, on land, however, not sea.

Within a short distance of our little island there was another – Hayling Island – and despite the country being war weary, there was a group of adventurous souls who relieved their boredom by setting up a nudist colony. Entrance to their enclave was strictly forbidden, but hovering helicopters didn't go through gates, they soared above them. One of our pilots, at least did exactly that, flying slowly, scanning the nudists from above and allegedly, picturing them. I was not privy to the workings of our higher echelons but the story goes that at least one of the culprits was disciplined.

I have no record, or knowledge, of what happened to the pictures. Destroyed? Kept as evidence? Your guess is as good as mine, but it was rumoured that they showed some outstanding images. Pilots, being naturally men who faced risks in the course of their duties, had another habit, 'Buzzing' or low flying over places they knew or to impress someone. One of 'my' pilots, Lt Lawrence, was a man who was a stickler for doing things properly so it was a considerable surprise to his ground crew when he was disciplined for 'buzzing'. He had apparently, decided to let his folks in the West Country know he was around and flew his Mosquito low over their house several times.

Problem was that no matter the pride his parents had in him, neighbours weren't as happy at being blasted with the roar of powerful Rolls Royce engines and forcibly objected to the disturbing of their peace.

Result – a reprimand for the lieutenant.

One or two other memories from Thorney persist. We had a squadron football team and for some reason, having been not too bad a full back, I was drafted into it as a centre-forward. Even more surprising was the fact that I started scoring goals like a forerunner of Jimmy Greaves or Denis Law. This led to a game which was a trial for the Fleet Air Arm XI. I was in direct opposition to an Army officer who played football as a second choice to rugby. Hardly had the game started when his lunging tackle smashed into my ankle, which immediately ballooned up. I was carried off, rushed to Chichester Hospital and the leg, from knee to toe, was put in plaster. I was due two weeks leave and a few days were added first, because I was 640 miles from my home in Elgin and second because I had 'won' some allowance for my injury.

Back home after a huge train journey involving three changes and a lot of pain and discomfort, I reached Elgin. Having had football injuries before, I took a couple of days rest then visited Bill Gordon. Bill had no medical qualifications as far as I knew, but he had magic hands. He also had a great thirst for the product of our glens and streams. When I called, he had obviously had a few, but was fully in control. I explained what had happened, showed him the plaster. Right away he cut it off with a pair of scissors the size of a couple of swords pinned together. The swelling was still there, the skin a mix of blue, yellow and purple.

He studied the mess for a few minutes, then began probing, pulling and twisting. It wasn't painless, but not too painful either. Even as I watched, the swelling subsided until it was just a thick ankle, not a rounded mess. I walked out of his house near Elgin Cathedral having handed him 5/- (25 pence) for his work. I was limping, but not nearly as badly as when I went in. Before the end of that leave I had been to a couple of dances. The ankle was tender, but that was all.

On my return to Chichester Hospital, the doctor who examined me was delighted with the treatment they had given me, though surprised that it had so completely done the trick. I didn't enlighten him – but it left me wondering about the magic some people, like Bill possessed to deal with other problems. I don't believe in the supernatural or such, but there is something special there and in the most unlikely packages.

Chapter Four

Back to Civvy Street

My time in the Fleet Air Arm was drawing to a close. I was a civilian who had been called up, not a serviceman heading into civvy street, but to this day some scattered memories survive of a period in my life which helped me in many ways.

There was the navy collar. It hung down the back of the neck. When you had to put on your great-coat the collar had to be held down, so that it would not end in a crumpled state and get you into trouble with various grades of disciplinary people. How did you ensure that? You had the young lady with whom you had been dancing and dating, slip her hands and arms under your arms and hold down the collar. This, of course, led to extremely close body contact, a great starter for the rest of the evening! It wasn't nearly as much fun when you failed to get the co-operation of a young lady and had to ask one of your mates to do the job. That had failure written all over it.

Normal trousers have a crease down the front. If you want to go 'tiddly', to use the naval expression for getting a bit flash, you ironed your navy trousers down the seams and inside out – giving a sort of figure of eight view – then added the extra. This meant ironing creases parallel to the ground, seven of them, to represent the seven seas.

First time I went home I decided to get really tiddlied up for my visit to a local dance. I couldn't remember any navy men being in or around Elgin, so I reckoned I'd be welcomed by the local girls. As always, my mother said she would look after the ironing, and she did. However, she was not au fait with the navy style and ironed them civvy fashion with the creases down the front! She was so willing I couldn't hurt her, so I managed to get my father to distract her and did the conversion job. End of story? Not quite. As I swanned up the street in my flash gear I spotted a navy uniform, then another, then to crown it all, a shore patrol looking for any navy man stepping out of line.

I hurried back home, changed in to my civvy sports jacket and flannels and found out from my father that they had forgotten to tell me the Fleet Air Arm had taken over from the Royal Air Force at Lossiemouth. I had a very quiet night at the dance, getting mostly the usual question – not so much "great to see you, Ian," more "when you go back then?" A bit soul destroying, to say the least.

I enjoyed most of my time in the Services and subscribe to the view that the yobs who pollute our day to day living now would benefit from a spell under a disciplinary chief petty officer or his equivalent in the army or RAF. I was no yob, but certainly learned self discipline in the service – if you didn't life was hell and the disciplinary folk made it so. But my relatively brief two years-plus time as a member of His Majesty's Forces was coming to an end and the future beckoned.

Stay in? No chance, even though we were given a talk by a British Airways bloke who said there were vacancies in his organisation for air mechanics, other than armourers that is!! At least one lad took him up on it and, I believe, had a successful career with several civilian airlines, but it wasn't for me or the great majority of us.

I had done a few small jobs for a local paper in Chichester and a lady I was told was on the management side suggested I could join their staff as a reporter. All my life, though, I have found that true perspective has come from getting back to my home town and looking at things from there. I was seeing a girl while stationed at Thorney Island, but it was more a case of couple of youngsters learning about that side of life rather than a wedding-bells-round-the-corner situation.

So back home to Elgin I went knowing that because I had been called up, my job with The Northern Scott would be open to me on my return. More than ever I wanted to be a reporter and it seemed common sense.

What I didn't know at the time was that the next six years were to define the rest of my life.

* * *

I bounced out of the service full of optimism and confidence and just in time for Christmas and New Year 1947. The world was my oyster and to add to my enjoyment I had a demobilisation gratuity of about £100 – a lot of money back then. Not only that, but I had hardly settled back with my mother, father and young brother Ron in Elgin than another similar sum landed in my possession. Had they paid me only half what I was due first time or, had I received a double payment by mistake? I didn't check . . . just accepted that for the first time in my life I had money to burn! And burn it I did.

Two colours had ruled my life up until then – blue and grey. That was the extent of variation in any outer clothing I could afford. Don't forget also that, much though I liked the uniform, my navy gear was coloured, understandably navy. So my first purchase with my new-found wealth was a coat of many colours. I bought it in Hepworths of Elgin, where a friend of my father's was manager. It was in the shop window when I first saw it, a glorious, basically light coloured raglan style winter weight with flecks of all sorts of colours worked into the fabric. It stood out for me like a beacon among the dark and dreary coloured clothes around it. By memory it cost me £8 – and I saw one vaguely similar in a shop window recently priced at over £200. No, I wasn't tempted to buy that one!

And the rest of the cash windfall? Confession time . . . most of it went on having a few nips (whisky) and pints (beer) with the lads.

Everywhere up and down the country young men and not-so-young had come flooding out of the services and back into civvy street. Back to wives, to girl friends, to previously held jobs, to a quiet life compared to the horrors some had suffered, to fun and games for others. I tended towards the latter, being only 20 years of age and rich by standards of the time. What if I had been shrewd and clever and invested the money? I'd obviously have had few financial worries in the future. But I didn't – and I don't have one single regret, oh well – one, of which more later.

Back in my job as a reporter with the *Northern Scot* –after a month's holiday at home and mostly playing football, going to three or four dances a week or having a drink – I settled quickly. New pals and old we enjoyed ourselves. My local was The Crown Bar in Elgin's Batchen Street.

Pointing the way to the future, though I didn't know it, I covered football on Saturday's – mostly Elgin City and Lossiemouth in the Highland League – for my paper and *The Sunday Post* in Dundee. That was great, but it meant that by the time I had written my reports and filed them over the phone, I didn't arrive at the pub until about three rounds after the others had started. This meant that while they had a steady intake, I had to rush down a couple of quick ones to catch up and you know what the consequences of rushing drink can have! I didn't get into any serious trouble, but didn't enjoy things like the dancing as much as I might have and my parents certainly didn't enjoy me stumbling into the house at all hours.

But that doesn't explain the 'why' of the situation. Why I wanted a coat of many colours was obvious . . . but why the excessive drinking by so many ex servicemen, who hadn't necessarily been heavy drinkers before and during their service time?

When I got over it I began to look for an answer and it didn't take long to come up with one. For years we had been shouted and sworn at by men with a badge on their arm, a stripe or two or even a 'pip' or two on their shoulder indicating an officer. Some were OK, others morons glorying in the power to shout, scream and swear at you knowing you couldn't answer back. We weren't 'regulars' who were looking at a career in the Services but young men called up to serve their country. That we didn't mind but we did object to the way we were treated by the morons!

So out we came into a life where, if you had bad bosses, you could answer back, speak freely, move on to something else. The relief I believe showed in an independence of spirit and the tendency to have a few more drinks than was sensible. I have no regrets about my service time. I met people who became good friends; I learned there were different ways of life in different parts of the country and different values. But it took a long time to forget the abusive and often plain ignorant men who did all the shouting at you.

Among the regular Saturday night drinkers in The Crown were some fascinating characters. Bob Combe, for instance. Robert F Combe, to give him his full title, was a local solicitor and gay. I had come across one or two in the services who were that way inclined, men and women, but somehow never expected it in my hometown. Later I found that there was a crowd of them, but that realization came a long time later.

Bob didn't bother us with that side of his life, he knew the answer he would have received had he tried, but he enjoyed drinking with us and joining in the banter. Always out to impress, just in case the impressed were willing to be more than just friendly, he would knock back drinks that made the rest of us shudder. I particularly remember a concoction of crème de menthe, brandy and whisky which disappeared in a flash. Often we had to carry him out to a waiting taxi, but there he would be next time round sitting on his favourite seat at the bar. What I haven't mentioned so far is that he was also a genius in his own profession!

Anyone committing a crime in the area and due to appear in court tried desperately to retain his services as their defender. Big cases and small, he took them all in his stride and as I watched him in action in court I couldn't help wondering how this could be the same man as the Saturday night drunk.

A simple enough case proved his ability to me. This particular 'travelling man' had been up before the magistrates and Sheriff on scores of occasions. He had been found guilty of assault, drunkenness and a dozen other low level crimes – low level in the sense that the troubles usually involved only people, like himself, who were court regulars. Always he had pleaded guilty and the punishment ranged from fines to spells in prison.

This time though, he pleaded not guilty to an assault on his female partner, allegedly his wife, but no proof of this could be found. We in the press seats couldn't believe it until we realised Bob Combe was defending. Now we were guaranteed some fun.

And on went the trial, with several witnesses seemingly building up an unbreakable case against the accused. The defence solicitor asked few questions, so few that we wondered if he had at last bitten off more than he could chew. The only thing we noticed was that the witnesses to the alleged beating the 'wife' had suffered were members of her family or associates of the family, but that was more or less expected. Finally we came to the last witness, one of the couple's daughters.

Usually a tomboy type, careless with looks and clothes, she was demurely dressed in a clean, neat frock, her hair carefully combed, her face and hands shiningly clean. She said she was with her mother in the caravan on the night in question, when her father came in screaming abuse, threatening and then attacking her mum. He only stopped when she somehow managed to pull him away. After that he ran off into the night and she called neighbours in and the police were sent for.

Not much doubt there, then.

As he rose to question the young lady, Mr Combe seemed more interested, more alert than previously. He carefully went over her evidence, in which she never deviated from her previous description of the events.

"And at what time did all this start," asked Mr Combe.

"Exactly ten minutes to eleven that night," was the reply.

"Why are you able to be so accurate?"

"Because he had done it before and I knew I'd be asked times and things, so I looked at the clock."

"A clock like the one in the court here?"

"Well, a bit like it."

"So what is the time on this clock?"

A moment's silence, then, from the witness box a sob.

"Take your time, young lady," said the Sheriff.

Another sob and a few tears. We all waited patiently, though I did notice one or two of the witnesses had quietly filed out of the court room. Finally,

"I don't know," came from the witness, followed by a flood of tears.

Mr Combe was patient. He waited for the tears to subside. Then asked quietly,

"You can't write and certainly can't tell the time? This whole tale is a lie and you are the key to that lie by pretending to know the time and establish the so-called 'facts' of an assault your father was never guilty of."

That was it. The whole story came out. Her mother had been seeing another man, he had a short temper and, on the night in question, the couple had fallen out, with the man lashing out at her mother. She, the daughter had got out of bed and seen him disappear before helping her mother.

But why the deception? It appears the mother had long wanted rid of the husband, the current accused, but had been frightened he would turn really nasty if he learned he had been 'replaced' in her affections, so she dreamed up a plot with her 'witnesses' and especially her daughter who, though not simple, was easily led.

The accused was freed, the actual assailant later charged . . . with Bob Combe politely refusing to appear on his behalf because of previously arranged business! Not much of a case in the grand order of things maybe, but proof of the skill of a solicitor, who treated the impossible as possible. And what happened to him? He became British chess champion, he moved to Aberdeen and into maritime law, possibly the most complicated of all branches of the profession . . . and later committed suicide.

What a waste, what a sad ending.

It was a motley crew who had their Saturday night drinking session in The Crown. The common denominator was probably football and one among us was a good example of all that was best on the ball. Tony G had magic in his feet, but never really exploited it because he was a rogue who didn't believe in hard work – and that included training and making sacrifices to improve his ability. Though his admirers at club level were many, they all shied off in the end because of that flaw in his make-up.

In the early days of our association with Tony he was just 'one of the lads' who entered easily into the Saturday night chat and often went with us afterwards to 'the dancing' where he was as adept on the dance floor as he was on the football field.

So, nothing to worry about there then – until a cold winter night, that is.

"I've won, I've won . . . " he shouted again and again. And when we finally got to look at the paper it was a football coupon – the ten results part. Against all of Tony's forecasts was a tick and a result. They were all correct. Discussion raged. It was established that the week before the ten results had paid out a hefty four figure sum (remember this was 1947) so Tony was going to be a rich man.

The drink flowed – none of it paid for by Tony. When he said he was heading south to visit his sister, who was having some personal problems he added that he was a "bit short of cash for the journey," but would try and get an advance from his boss "on Monday."

"No problem" said we generous drink-fuelled mates, "we'll have a whip-round and you can be off as soon as you like."

We knew his sister, who had married an English soldier during the war, so everything was above board. Tony was finally handed a three figure sum of money, over half of it subscribed by Bob Combe, the solicitor who was ever generous to good causes. Eventually Tony was off into the night – and that was the last time any of us, to my knowledge ever saw him.

Apparently, unbeknown to us and some time before, he had decided to leave Elgin for pastures new. He didn't have the money to make the move so dreamed up the coupon scam. He had waited until the football results were read out on the radio, then carefully filled in the appropriate scores and ticks to 'prove' that he had a winning line. After that it had been the jaunt into The Crown – leaving it until we'd had a few drinks – and the revelation about his success on the coupon. What followed went exactly to his plan!

His sister was contacted some time later, via solicitor Combe and all she could say was that she was having a very happy family life, that we should have known Tony was a crook and that she hadn't heard from him in years. Where is he, or was he? I have no idea and with the passing of years my annoyance is more on the nature of a wry smile now and again at the thought of how we were so easily conned, and absorbing the lesson that, if something seems to be too good to be true, it probably is!

Meanwhile life as a reporter went on. By now I had graduated to the big stuff, town and county council meetings, political rallies, the Sheriff

Court, rather than the Police and Sheriff Court time about, murders, robberies, farm gossip, in fact everything which involves a local reporter.

I particularly liked the County Council. Moray and Nairn is an area rich in rich people, who probably still look on ordinary decent folk as lesser beings as they certainly did in the pre and post-war years. Typical were Miss Wharton Duff and the laird of Pitgaveny, Brander Dunbar.

Miss Wharton Duff once took me outside her country home after an interview, pointed a hillside of trees and said in her near masculine voice, "These Wheeler, could earn me more than you will probably earn in a life-time, now make sure you have every word of our interview correct." She was an imposing thick-set figure in her Harris tweed hat and twin set, brogues and heavy woollen or lisle stockings, all set off by brooches and rings which certainly looked worth big money and strings of pearls that definitely were.

No more imposing than the wee laird, though. He was about as broad as he was tall and topped by a round head and a crew cut many years before they became the fashion of the day. He had a Kaiser-type (leader of the German nation in the First World War) look enhanced by a heavy moustache, wore again, heavy tweed clothes, including a kilt and smoked a vile looking curved pipe filled with a choking, heavy duty tobacco.

And they hated one another's guts! No matter to what Miss Wharton Duff raised in meeting of the County Council, he objected, always with a heavy lacing of sarcasm. As he was a noted ladies man, I often wondered if she, in her younger days had spurned his advances and this was his revenge. Mind you, the more I looked at her, the more I eased away from that thought!

Matters came to a head when she proposed a motion that smoking be banned in council chambers. The laird of course smoked before, during and after meetings, causing much coughing and spluttering among those around him. But the more they protested the more he smoked. Miss Wharton Duff brought things to a head with her proposal. After due deliberation and much muttering from the laird, the motion was approved. Without preamble he rose from his seat, strode towards her and blew a huge cloud of smoke straight into her face muttering seeming profanities between puffs. To her credit, she didn't succumb, breaking into a smile of triumph as he departed the meeting. I can't recall him returning.

Though I was now really a local paper reporter with contacts galore and a routine which I knew by heart, this had in me an unsettling effect rather than a feeling that I had it made. It was compounded by my time in the Fleet Air Arm, when I had realised there was a big world outside the one I had known in the first 18 years of my life. I had nothing against my upbringing or my home town, but change beckoned. Not that it came quickly and it took an expenses row and a plane crash to really get it going.

The expenses business involved, would you believe 6d (2.5 pence). The Queen's nanny, Miss Mabel Anderson, had a sister who lived a few miles south of Elgin. A daily paper phoned to say Miss Anderson was having a brief holiday there and could we get a quote from her.

There was a bus service which ran past her sister's door, but the daily paper was in a hurry and no buses were available at a convenient time. So I hired a bicycle from a friend of my fathers, Tommy Hay whose business was selling, repairing and hiring them. Young and pretty fit, I cycled to a chat with Miss Anderson, who was charming but would only say she was having a quiet break with her sister in a lovely part of the world and didn't want to be disturbed. She would spend only a week at most before returning to her duties. It wasn't much but the daily was satisfied when I phoned it over with a sub-editor phoning back to say they hadn't expected anything quotable.

So, on the Friday, I entered 6d in my expenses for hire of the bicycle. On the Monday, I was called into the office of the editor (Stephen Young, senior) and told he couldn't approve the 6d. His line of questioning was, why didn't I take the bus? Why had I not used my own bicycle? I pointed out the bus times and explained that my bicycle was a rusting wreck lying in a corner of the shed at home. Still he wouldn't relent.

It was ridiculous and even though I did, reluctantly, receive the 6d two weeks later the injustice simmered because then, and on other occasions, little niggles cropped up about anything connected with money, including wages. Compounding my annoyance was the fact that the daily paper paid an astonishing £5 for the minimal interview, which went into a 'pool' shared by the editorial staff, so 6d from 1200d certainly wasn't much.

The other cause of a desire to move on began some eight years before when one the biggest stories to come out of my area in many a year happened. In May 1945 (four months before I was called up) a bomber from RAF Lossiemouth crashed down on a house in the town. There must have been hundreds of thousands of flights in and out of the airfield on the edge of town in the 70 or so years of it's existence, but amazingly, though flight paths skirted the populated area, few serious incidents are recorded.

This one was different. A bomber heading back to base crashed on a block of houses in Church Street and obliterated eight civilians – members of the Flood and Allan families – and three aircrew. It was a stunning blow for a tight-knit community and, of course, a major news story for journalists who flocked from far and wide to report on the event and the aftermath. As 'the local man' I was at the centre of the coverage then and when the massively attended funerals took place. For me, there was also a very special issue involved, one which extended beyond my service time.

For years I had been in contact with the Trantor family. Father, Mr Alex Trantor, had a licensed grocer's shop only yards from the crash site and in the family house next door was the only telephone in that part of town. In the days of mobile phones, laptop computers and the like this may seem strange. To send copy from football matches to the Sunday papers on a Saturday, I and other freelanced journalists had a 500 yards sprint from Lossiemouth Football Club's Grant Park to that phone the minute a home game ended. This led to considerable competition, but fortunately for me, one 'competitor' had asthma and the other was some 30 years older than both of us. As I was still young and fit and able to move quickly, I regularly got there first.

While I was phoning in my pre-Services days, courtesy of Mr and Mrs Trantor, I would see some young girls around the house. They were the daughters of the Trantor's, nice, neat and tidy, but far too young for a man of the world like me! By the time I returned to my reporting job and used the same telephone for such things as updates on the crashed aircraft story, a couple of them were women and I increasingly noticed a blonde-haired one with attractive looks and a lovely figure.

I found out her name was Mildred, courtesy of Mrs Trantor, both a well known local personality and a tremendous contact for the news for my paper. I also discovered that daughter Mildred sang with a local dance band which often played at dances in Elgin's Bishopmill Hall, a regular haunt of mine on a Saturday night. So, interest aroused, I went to the dance there with the specific idea of meeting the lovely lady. Unfortunately, I had met up with my drinking pals in town before setting off so, by the time I arrived at the hall I was not, shall we say, at my best.

It was actually the interval and as luck would have it, Mildred was outside having a breath of fresh air. The hall was packed, no more allowed in. I tried to persuade her to get in through a window – which I later found was the ladies toilet – but she understandably refused. So I waited and when some early leavers came out managed to talk my way in. I also managed a dance with Mildred and that, in 1948 was our first date. She was all that I had hoped for and seemed to like me and we 'got serious' with regular dates.

In September 1950, we married after the usual courtship of the time; cinema visits and dances, though I must admit she must have had doubts when she had to pay me into the cinema on our first date. By this time I was earning reasonable money but I was broke because I had 'blown' my services gratuity as well as my income, drinking with the lads and generally throwing money away. I corrected this and now, over sixty years on we are still together so, after a shaky start, I must have got something right.

The wedding was in St Geraldine's Church, still there at the top of the cliff face in Lossiemouth, with the reception (costing £53/06d) in the long-gone Gordon Arms Hotel, Elgin and the honeymoon in Inverurie,

50 miles away. We reached there by taxi on the September 14 wedding night which seems a bit tame now when you read about current honeymoons in the West Indies, the Maldives and so on, but it was fairly normal in those times.

The £53-plus consisted of 83 lavish dinners costing a total of £35/5/6d; refreshments £14/2 shillings; a special license for serving alcoholic drinks, 10/-; changing rooms 10/6d; fruit squash for those not wanting alcoholic drinks, 7/6d and 90 teas for 2/5/-. There was also the wedding cake at £6/6/-; the hire of buses from the wedding in Lossiemouth to the reception in Elgin, £5; and sundry other expenses like the wedding announcement in 'my' newspaper (for which I got a staff rebate!) at 9/2d and the cost of invitations, cake bags and so on for the 83 wedding guests and 17 more at the evening dance. I read the other day of a not too special wedding in England costing £18,000, so even with inflation we didn't do too badly, especially as I earned as their local correspondent, £5 from the licensed trade paper, *The National Guardian*, for reporting the wedding of the daughter of a licensed grocer!

Our first home was a flat rented out by a local taxi driver and his wife. At harvest time especially we had as fellow occupants so many mice from an adjacent field that we swear they played five-a-side mouse football when we were trying to sleep. There was also an outside lavatory – well outside! Downstairs, outside into the main street, then round the back of the house. None too enjoyable on cold winter nights, or for that matter, any night.

Things did improve after a few months when we moved into a two-roomed house two streets away. It still had an outside lavatory, but it was much nearer and straight out from the back door. Do you wonder that today, when we have a fully-fledged bathroom AND en-suite toilet and shower room we feel in the lap of luxury? Though we settled pretty smoothly into married life, that itch grew to move on to try pastures new and to see how I would fare in a bigger arena.

My new wife had never travelled further than Aberdeen, but she was bravely willing to go with my wishes. It did not please her mother and though Mrs T and I remained friends, the atmosphere chilled a bit. Her reason for disappointment was that it was the first 'break' in the family. All other six children were in Lossiemouth, though in later years all bar one eventually moved to other places.

Chapter Five

Why I Joined
DC Thomson

. . . but back to my change of job.

The DC Thomson group contacted me during an annual visit by *Sunday Post* editor John Martin, *Weekly News* editor Alf Anderson and Henry Cook and I told them how we felt. Also in the frame was the *Aberdeen Press and Journal,* where most Northern Scot reporters went when they decided to move. Interviews were arranged with both and my first call was Aberdeen.

Exactly on the time I was scheduled to be interviewed by a Mr Veitch, the editorial manager, a well dressed woman strode in and, without hesitation, opened the door of his office and entered, closing the door behind her. To say I was not best pleased is a total understatement. Fifteen minutes later, 15 minutes after I was supposed to be interviewed, I walked out and caught the next train back to Elgin.

A day later, Mr Veitch phoned to ask where I had been, I told him, then added that I did not take kindly to making an arrangement, travelling a 128 miles round trip to keep it, only to find I took second place to an obviously chance-taking visitor. "But that was Lady Tweedsmuir," (who I think, was a director at the time) he said in a sort of hushed and reverential voice. I will not say exactly what I replied but it all ended with both of us slamming the telephone down and, when we met once some time later, ignoring one another completely. *(As a post-script to that incident, it is interesting to note that now the* Press and Journal *is owned by the firm I did join, D C Thomson).*

The next step was to arrange an interview with Mr Henry Cook, editorial manager of D C Thomson. The contrast was amazing. I arrived in Dundee where a hotel room had been booked. A slight hitch occurred when I realised the special shirt I was to wear for the interview didn't have buttoned sleeves. Instead I needed a pair of cuff links, which I hadn't brought with me. So it was a quick dash to the nearest (and, I found out later, most expensive) jewellers in town and a parting of the ways between me and £4.10/-. However, the rest of the day went well. I arrived on time, was interviewed on time, had a cup of tea and a biscuit during the chat with Mr Cook – but walked out without agreeing to a move.

Sticking point was the fact that, as well as my wages back home I had a share of the freelance 'pool' and I felt the wage difference wasn't enough. Again, a quick decision. I was only yards from the office on my way back to the railway station when I was asked to return. I did, 10/- (50p) per week was added to my starting wage and I agreed to join the firm I was to spend the rest of my working life with. It was February, 1953 and I was 25 years of age and two years and five months married.

It can't be said that I had an auspicious start. I went straight into the *Courier and Advertiser* (as it was then known) news desk, charged with allocating photographers jobs all over the circulation area of Dundee, Angus, Perth, Fife and so on. The trouble was I simply did not know the area, had never been in it before. So it was back to Mr Cook after a very few months and a request to join the reporters on the *Courier* and *Evening Telegraph*. He rightly pointed out that news editor was higher up the pecking order than being one of a large team of reporters. However, all my working life I believed that position wasn't as important as job satisfaction. While I was out of my depth on the news desk and my wife was suffering from my discontent, I knew what I was doing as a reporter after 11 years, minus service time, in the job. Again, full marks to the decision makers in the firm. They took on board my plea and within weeks I was a reporter again.

The re-start was not easy! First thing senior reporter Stuart Adamson said to me when we talked was, "No one is a real reporter unless they have been trained here." He was wrong and must have relented because, in a short time, with my verbatim shorthand and pretty fast typing speed, I was covering big court cases and meetings which were to lead to the creation of Dundee's now highly acclaimed University, of which the directors of D C Thomson were solidly in favour.

In the short time before this though, interesting things happened. I covered a police court case where one of the many charged with offences was a ravishing looking red-head who had been soliciting the night before. I barely noted the case as there was a regular flow of them and they weren't all that newsworthy. As I left the court, however, a sharply dressed man wearing a traditional soft hat of the day and an oversized woollen coat approached me, the red head a step or two behind him.

Was I "the Tele reporter?"

"Yes."

Naming the girl he went on "Her uncle is in the Royal Canadian Mounted Police and if her case goes in the paper it will affect his career."

I couldn't believe what I was hearing. Did the Dundee evening paper circulate widely in the northern wilds of Canada? Who in the Mounties was going to read the item? And the local paper seldom reported such cases anyway. Then came the punch-line, presumably because he was worried by my silence.

" . . . and if you keep it out I'll see to it you have a session with her yourself."

Generous or what? By this time I had absorbed what was being said, but again his impatience go the better of him.

" . . . and if it does go in I'll see to it that you are sorted out."

That was it. As a reporter, insults are not infrequent, especially from low-life like this. Threats however, are a different thing. In similar language to that he was using, I told him to leave the scene, along with his 'friend.' We glared at one another for a minute, and then they went, with parting words which are not normal in polite company.

Returning to the office, I reported the incident to the editor, Mr Ralph Pryde. That night the evening paper carried three lines about the 10/- fine imposed on the girl. I never actually saw her minder again, but one night, around 1am when I was making a last check on 'anything happening in town'. At a city centre coffee stall, the owner said "There's a bloke looking for you" and described him. It fitted my police court pal (?) exactly. Stupidly, because by this time I had knowledge that he had been known to use a knife when trouble happened, I went looking for him. Luckily for me, I didn't find him and that was the end of one of the most bizarre episodes in my reporting life.

There was one other less serious event in Dundee which I have never forgotten. Having to hire a taxi one night so that my wife and I could get home from a party, I met this driver called Bob. I bumped into him several times after that and we got on well. His stories were really funny and the one that topped my list was about a 'lady of the night' Bob had regular contact with – in the strictly business sense, I mean.

"She took a shine to me after I ran her home one night" said Bob, who had a cheery face and an outlook on life and, like so many taxi drivers, was a great philosopher.

"A couple of days later the boss called me into his office and told me I would be her regular driver – whether I was on duty or not. So what I did for a long time after that, until she 'retired' really, was take her order to collect a gentleman – she never called them anything else and they were, in many cases, well known and prosperous – and take him up to her flat in one of the city's housing estates. This was her business premises; she had a house in a much better area.

"When I got there I had to look up to the window facing the road. If the curtains were drawn I had to do a tour round until they were opened. Drawn, it meant her client had taken longer to . . . um . . . clear the premises than she thought; open and the coast was clear for the next gentleman. I often had the bonus of taking the previous visitor back to the city and collecting the fare and a nice tip as well, not to mention additional cash from the lady at Christmas, New Year and Easter.

"As a post-script I was invited to her funeral some years later even though I had left the taxis. It was some party and it was there I learned that she had maintained a 'beat' in the city centre when she moved up-market. As a parting gift she had bequeathed it to her daughter, along with the proceeds from hiring it out!"

Some lady, indeed.

Steelie

This was also about the time I entered the world of big-time football. I watched a few Dundee fixtures, but the only football I was allocated to cover for the evening paper, were junior games. On my way to see Downfield (a district of Dundee) this particular Saturday, I noticed sitting in front of me on the bus, a man wearing a Stetson, certainly not the normal head gear worn by Dundee males!

On leaving the bus at the Downfield stop, I introduced myself to him and asked if he was on holiday. It turned out that he was from America to where he had emigrated some years previously. He had also, he claimed, played for Downfield a few times before leaving the city. It all turned out to be true and he was greeted as an old friend by several ex-players and a couple of committee men once we got into the ground.

Not a big story but a neat personal one for the behind-the-scenes column in the 'Tele'. However, it was noticed by Alf Anderson, the man who at the time edited *The Weekly News* and oversaw the sports sections of that paper, and he was impressed. I didn't know this until much later but all of a sudden I was allowed to cover the evening paper reports on Dundee and Dundee United, which were unique in journalism in that they were written in the present tense. Dundee had press seats in the main grandstand, United a bench where reporters sat – and hard lines if it rained because then your 'copy', written in ink or pencil on cheap paper, became pretty nearly unreadable.

The great privilege of watching Dundee was that Billy Steel played for them. There were other outstanding players in the team; full back Bobby Ancell, wing-halves (the real name for midfield players) Alfie Boyd, Tommy Gallacher and especially Doug Cowie, who had he been a Rangers or Celtic man, would have won at least four times the 20 Scotland appearances he did make. Up front alongside Steel, were outside-right George (Pud) Hill, the bravest winger, other than Jimmy McEwan (Raith Rovers and Aston Villa), Mike Summerbee (Manchester City) and Johnny Morrissey (Everton), I was ever to see. Bobby Flavell, one of the British starts who was tempted to Columbia for big money in a 1950's 'scandal' that rocked the game here. The English maximum wage was £20 per week and though Scotland had no maximum that was mostly because (apart from Rangers and maybe Celtic) no club could afford the £20.

But it all came back down to Steelie. In a truly incredible piece of business in 1950, George Anderson, the bow-tie wearing director-manager of Dundee, paid £23,500 to Derby County for the player rated, at the time, the best in his position in Britain. The money was astronomical by the standards of the time. If you doubt how good Steel was, the fact is that he played for Great Britain against the Rest of The World in preference to a host of outstanding inside forwards in teams all over Britain – not least the Middlesbrough magician Wilf Mannion.

I recall former Dundee team-mate and sports columnist colleague Tommy Gallacher saying to me years later, "Steelie was a genius. He spotted openings quicker than anyone, passed better than anyone, could create goals better than anyone, and scored goals as well as anyone. Some said he was a bit slow. Over a thirty yard run maybe he could have been quicker, but he didn't need 30 yards, give him any space at all and he was lightening and round you before you could do a thing."

You may think I am pitching things a bit high but I believe the Steel signing was the best investment by anyone in a player in my 50 years association with the game. The only comparable impact was by Eric Cantona when he signed for Manchester United. Dundee was a small club compared with United and the money spent on Steel had relatively greater rewards.

Sadly, Steel lasted only four years with Dundee. His off-field drinking – shades of George Best and Jim Baxter to come – cutting short what should have been one of the greatest careers in the game. In those four years though, Steel added 12 Scotland caps to the 18 already won with Greenock Morton and Derby County. Dundee had Cup success and pulled in maximum crowds wherever they went, partly because of the quality of their play, but equally because people wanted to see a football genius in action.

The Scotland selectors (the seven club directors who chose the country's team in those days) never felt comfortable with him. Steel didn't pay them the respect they felt they deserved and on one unforgettable occasion they turned up en masse to see Dundee play Celtic. The idea was that, having indicated they thought Steel was maybe past his best and not an automatic choice, they would be proved correct.

Not this time though. Steel, who knew what the Selectors thought, gave Evans the run-around culminating in 'nutmegging' (flicking the ball between Evans' legs twice), then carefully crossing the ball for diminutive Bobby Flavell to jokingly go down on his knees and nod it into the net. The seven wise (?) men departed Dens. They had arrived wondering whether to select Steel. They left with his name the first on the team sheet. Strangely enough that wasn't the end of my involvement with the Steel story.

When I was moved to Glasgow office I became friendly with an inside forward called Joe Roy, an outstanding junior performer with Clydebank, now a senior team and star of Scotland's junior representative team. During a chance meeting in Glasgow city centre, he told me he was on his way to meet George Anderson, the same Dundee boss who had signed Steel.

"Seems," said Joe, "they want me as a replacement for Billy Steel."

A hotel near Queen Street station was the meeting place and I got there not long after Joe. Sitting quietly near the entrance/exit main door I kept an eye on everyone arriving or leaving. And suddenly bow-tied George Anderson was in my sights. Naturally, we knew one another from Dundee days and he barely hesitated before charging over to me.

"Get out of this hotel" he shouted, his face red with anger. "No press men are allowed in here . . . "

As I was going to be polite and discuss the Roy situation with him calmly when the opportunity arose, this riled me.

"Don't talk rubbish," I said, "you know and I know that I have every right to be here and if you don't want to talk about the Roy signing then I'll move out and write the story anyway."

That calmed him – slightly. How did I know what was happening? He would sort out whoever told me.

As it was my pal Joe himself, I didn't want him getting into trouble so I replied that by an amazing coincidence I was in the hotel to see a football contact, had arrived early to have a coffee and saw both Roy and a Dundee director I knew arriving. The steam had stopped coming out of his ears by this time, he shrugged his shoulders and asked what I wanted to know. It was downhill from there. I got my story, including an interview with Joe Roy, to whom I introduced myself as if we had never met before!

Bobby Moore – 'captain cool' but did he
enjoy playing at Anfield?

Denis Law, goal scorer supreme, although there
was one goal he didn't want to score. Note the Law
trademark – fingers gripping the jersey cuffs.

Narey, the supreme professional, but he
didn't always agree with referees!

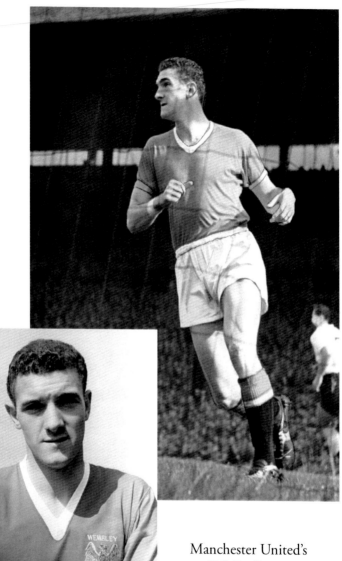

Manchester United's
Bill Foulkes –
bravery and quiet
celebration.

A Ranger's and Scotland legend – Jim Baxter.

Two Tottenham Hotspur 'giants' – Alan Gilzean (left) a scorer
and provider of goals with Dundee and Spurs manager Bill
Nicholson, who built outstanding teams at White Hart Lane.

Just after his sensational transfer to Dundee,
Billy Steel strolls out of Dens Park.

David Narey (see also picture 3).

Manager of what is reckoned the greatest
Leeds United team ever – Don Revie.

Centre-half Paul Hegarty, captain of
Dundee United in their great years.

The inimitable Bobby Charlton in full flight
– a scary experience for defenders.

Bill Shankly's wife Nessie enjoys a cuppa. The wives
of football folk used to be low profile, but were
still vital to their husband's success.

Chapter Six

Glasgow . . .
Our First Real Home

There is an argument constantly going on about Glasgow being a better place to live than Edinburgh and vice versa.

Having lived in Glasgow and worked a lot in Edinburgh I would say Scotland is privileged to have two cities of this stature with all their differences. Instead of argument there should be delight; though that is the view of a neutral definitely not shared by the respective populations! So, because a major D C Thomson office was there, Glasgow was where Mildred and I settled – and we loved it.

A two bedroom flat in Shawlands on the south side was our base, and our first real home in that we had always had rented rooms before. OK it was up three flights of stairs, but it was a home where we could shut the front door and be ourselves. As time passed it became even more of a home with our daughter Laura Margaret being born in the bedroom of number 46 Walton Street – with my wife even now keeping up her complaint that, as she lay in the throes of childbirth I was making chips and a cup of tea for the (attractive) midwife.

Son Graeme was born in a nursing home, still on the south side, and his arrival gave us our first real fright in our married life. Out of hospital, Mildred developed a pulmonary embolism, where blood clots caused major problems in her thigh and, worse still, in a lung. As the ambulance men rushed her to Mearnskirk hospital, our doctor, Dr Isbister, said quietly to me, "Everything should be all right with treatment Ian, but you must also realise that the worst could happen as this is a serious medical condition."

Six weeks were to pass before Mildred left hospital, weak but back with us again. Laura had been looked after by Mildred's elder sister Ella and Graeme by younger sister Mae – in Lossiemouth, 200-plus miles north. While our home life was developing like this, I was trying to get on top of my working life, but finding things strangely difficult.

Finally I had to go to the doctor. After tests I was diagnosed as having a kidney problem caused by a tube leading from bladder to kidney being too narrow. The kidney was gradually being destroyed. So it was into Victoria Infirmary, a short distance from our home and a six hour operation conducted by Doctors Chapman and Sutherland. I had scores of stitches inside and outside my body when the operation was finished and was off work for some three months.

Describing the operation to students at my bedside, Mr Chapman, by memory a tall balding man, summed it up thus, while holding up an X-ray, "this one went well . . . we chopped off a bit there, popped in some plastic and he'll be as right as rain soon." I was told some time later that my op was only the third ever attempted – and the other two men died! I was also told that if I am buried when I die, the plastic will still be there when the rest is dust! Then, to crown it all, within a year I was back in the Victoria Infirmary.

I have always loved pancakes, especially those made by Mildred. On this occasion, coming home late from a football match I saw a fresh batch had been baked. Stupidly I piled on syrup and ate a few. During the night I woke with a searing pain in my stomach. Dr Isbister was called, immediately diagnosed appendicitis and I was in the infirmary within an hour. Appendix removal followed and 10 days later I was out, and thankfully didn't take long to get back into full working order.

Yes, a period in life which tested us seriously but which we thankfully survived, strengthened as so often happens by setbacks.

* * *

I wondered when I returned to work how I would cope . . . and the first thing that happened didn't inspire particular confidence. I was asked by editorial office Chief Sandy Reid to join him for a chat.

"We have decided that in view of your health problems to move you from *The Weekly News* to *The People's Journal*," he said.

Impatiently I butted in with, "That's hardly fair, I'm fit and healthy – healthier than I've been for a long time and working on my fitness."

He listened patiently before carrying on as if I hadn't spoken, "Which means you will be working on your own (The PJ was printed in Dundee, where sports editor Bob Miller was based), have use of a car, and get a ten per cent increase in your wages. Apart from special requests from the editor (Jimmy Hood, the best I ever worked with) or the sports editor you will set your own agenda and choose your own games to attend."

What must first be appreciated is that *The Weekly News* had much the bigger circulation of the two and it had been a dream of mine to work for it since I was a young lad. I was only one of four or five sports writers on it, attending games depended on how the sports editor decided. It didn't take me long to delete my objections and say OK to the switch and that turned out to be one of the best decisions of my working life.

I had enjoyed The Weekly News – Sunday Post years but here I was being offered, if you like, my own personal niche where I could express myself, not work to a formula set by others. I still had a sports editor, but he was of the type who preferred not to interfere if things were going well. In four years we never had a cross word so he must have been happy with my contributions.

I had been boxing correspondent for both the weekly and Sunday papers and I did miss this, but there are always pluses and minuses when life changes direction. A few particular boxing incidents will remain with me forever, though. For example . . . Peter Keenan was a Glasgow lad with considerable talent in the boxing ring. A bantamweight, 8st 7lbs then, he was about 5ft 4ins tall and his dark, curly hair topped a cheeky Scottish-type face, which thickened through the punches he took in his career, but never really lost a youthful look. He reached Empire bantamweight championship success and it really meant something in the 1950's because Britain had an Empire then and it produced many good fighters.

On this particular occasion, Peter was reaching the end of his career and was being faced, in an open-air fight at Partick Thistle's football ground, Firhill Park, by a challenger from just outside Glasgow called Johnny Smillie.

Slim and as fair as Peter was dark, Smillie was a more than adequate opponent, managed by the shrewd and experienced Tommy Gilmour, father of Scotland's well known promoter today, and also named Tommy Gilmour with the addition of junior to indicate the dynasty.

The first few rounds were embarrassing – for Keenan's supporters. Peter barely laid a glove on his opponent and in return, took a succession of punches, never quite lethal enough to knock him out but cumulatively sufficient for us, watching at ringside and reporting on the fight, to reckon it wouldn't be long before the champion was and ex-champion.

As they left their corners for the fifth round, Peter was obviously struggling and had red weal's from punches and the ropes more or less all over his body while Smillie looked as cool, calm and collected as if he was about to start the fight. At first the round went like all the others – Smillie attacking, Keenan hanging on. Then came what looked like the end. Keenan was bullied onto the ropes just above my press seat and Smillie moved in for the kill. As he swung his arm to let go with the final punch, the challenger made his first mistake of the night. In his youthful enthusiasm to land the coup de grâce, he left his chin undefended for the first time and it proved fatal.

Keenan was a veteran, had seen it all, done it all and knew when to take advantage of a mistake. His fist thudded into Smillie's jaw, the impact being even greater than normal because the challenger was moving in onto the blow. Down he went like a sack of potatoes, out for the ten counts before he hit the canvas.

Keenan's supporters went berserk; Smillie's sat stunned in their seats. When the referee held up Keenan's arm to signal victory the still-champion could barely raise a smile, never mind a victory dance.

In the loser's dressing room afterwards, Tommy Gilmour swiped his hand down Smillie's back. "He isn't even sweating." He shouted at the assembled reporters, "He won the fight because it should have been stopped long before it finished." He went on and on this theme until a reporter, who had to get out and write his piece, reminded him, "Say what you like, Tommy, but the record books will only say 'Smillie, KO'd round five.' That's all folk in years to come will know." Things suddenly went quiet . . .

The sequel was personal to me. As my newspaper's boxing correspondent I had to look for an angle which the daily and evening papers hadn't covered (I represented a weekly and a Sunday) and took the decision to write and tell Keenan, 'It's time to retire . . . you can't go on taking beatings like this . . . let's remember the good years, the winning fights, your prime."

On the Monday of the next week the phone on my desk rang. "Somebody wants to see you at the front desk," I was told. So down the one flight of stairs I went to see a very, very irate Keenan glaring at me from the other side of the counter.

"Who says I'm finished," he yelled, "you and your bloody reports . . . I'd better not meet you outside, pal."

He went on in this vein for a few minutes before I could get a word in and I don't know how I remained cool enough to reply with, "Don't forget your hands are lethal weapons, so hit me and you are in real trouble." Cowardice or common sense – I leave you to judge, but it worked. He calmed down some and suddenly about turned and slammed his way out the entrance door to the office.

A further episode between him and me happened only days later. I went to his home in Glasgow's west end to talk about my article but he was out and his charming wife made me a cup of tea while we waited for his return. When I ran out of waiting time he still hadn't returned. All very innocent and business-like, but he didn't see it that way. At a later boxing event, his anger at me obviously still simmering, he tried to accuse me of deliberately visiting his wife when he was out, with all the inferences that cast. This was nonsense and this time I was angry and made it abundantly clear to him that he was being stupid. We parted – and never met again.

Glasgow's boxing scene threw up some other interesting moments. Scotland's two leading Sunday papers, the *Sunday Post* and *Sunday Mail*, occupied ringside seats at Kelvin Hall shows, of which there were many during my time. Because more or less the same folk occupied those seats every time, it appeared that the ringside gambling fraternity trusted us. So when bets were laid on the result of fights, the round they would end, the punch that would finish it and so on, the money would be brought forward and laid in front of us; and the roll was sometimes big enough to choke the proverbial horse.

The carrier was often a small dark-haired bloke, with black, dead-looking eyes. I honestly admit that I seldom looked his way. He was like something that is on the edge of your awareness, but isn't important. So it came as a bit of a shock to find later that he was, in fact, called Peter Manuel, the same man who terrorised the city of Glasgow and around with a series of murders which saw him eventually being the last person hanged for his crimes in Scotland.

I was only one of many, many husbands who hated leaving the house at night during that period, but with the advent of floodlit football and boxing shows being night-time events I had to. I phoned home regularly and before I left, made sure our across-the-landing neighbours knew I was going out.

There was also the bomb incident! I had called on Tommy Gilmour at his Gorbals gymnasium on my way to now defunct football club third Lanark's Cathkin Park for a couple of interviews with players Dave Hilley and Matt Gray. The task completed it was back to the Gilmour gym . . . to be met by a typically huge Glasgow policeman of the time, asking "And what do you want, son?"

I explained that I was a Sunday Post sports writer going in to see Tommy Gilmour.

"Shouldn't tell you this, but a bomb's gone off in there," he said. "I'll say I didn't see you going in".

The *Sunday Post* had great influence then and it is a safe bet that the bobby and his family were regular readers. So in I went to find damage to a stairway. I spoke to several people, including Tommy Gilmour, but they all claimed the whole thing was a mystery. As they say in Glasgow, I thought "Aye, right" because I knew the undercurrent of jealousy that existed in the boxing fraternity. Therefore, my next port of call was to another member of that fraternity a fair bit away from the Gilmour gym, but still in Glasgow.

Nothing was ever proved about the explosion, which only caused mild structural damage to the staircase. I cannot name names, but found the man I spoke to extremely interested in knowing if there had been 'anything unusual happening in the city?' Normally we talked only boxing and a bit of football, but this time he wanted to know about 'anything in the news.' The more he persisted in this line of questioning, the more I was convinced that he either was behind the planting of the device or knew who was. However, as I say, as nothing was ever proved my view is purely personal but . . .

Chapter Seven

Two Glasgow 'Greats'

Despite my interest in boxing, my main work was as a football writer, match reports and more importantly interviews with people involved in the game, from tea ladies all the way through to top level players, managers and so on. My favourite club was the now long defunct third Lanark – and if more people had listened to our articles in *The Weekly News*, then the club might have still been in existence. When a Mr Hiddlestone took over running the Cathkin Park outfit, we hinted strongly that his long term idea was to close the football club and dispose of the ground and surrounds for housing. Mr H. went ballistic and threatened all sorts of legal action.

Our sports editor was John Rankine, suave, dapper, always sporting a thin moustache, always dressed in a suit and tie – and frightened of no one.

"You have verbatim shorthand," he said to me.

"Yes," I replied.

"Then get a notebook and drive me to Hiddlestone's house," he said (he didn't drive).

As we drove through Glasgow I got my instructions.

"Be ready to take notes as soon as he opens the door, doesn't matter what is said," I was told. So my notebook was in my left hand and pen in my right when the door opened. It was the man himself.

As John said, "I am sports editor of *The Weekly News*, the paper you are threatening to sort out," I was busy writing this down.

"What's he doing?" queried Hiddlestone.

"Making sure we get an accurate record of all you and I say because I don't trust what might be your interpretation," he was told, while I busily continued with my shorthand.

"Can he stop and let us have a private conversation," was the next Hiddlestone comment.

After a pause, I was told to stop meantime and wait in the car while the two men met in the house. I cannot therefore tell you what went on, but let's just say that John returned to the car with a smile on his face, the threat of any action against the paper never materialised – and Cathkin is now derelict. It didn't happen immediately after our 'conference' but it did happen and a much-loved club went to the wall.

Rangers and Celtic were, then and now, Glasgow's major clubs and in the 1950s and early 1960's the ascendancy was with Rangers. One of the many players I became friendly with was a centre-half who wore the opposite colours. For some reason or other he had been signed for Celtic from Llanehli in Wales; not the sort of place you expect top stars to emerge from. And he wasn't a top star. Heavily built and not particularly mobile he was rated no more than a 'useful' at the job of keeping opposing strikers quiet. Two things made him a bit different, though.

He was the best player I ever saw at clearing a ball with his thigh. The heavy leather ball of those days would come spiralling down, pass the height for heading, and drop towards a booted clearance. But just as the opposition prepared to pounce on what looked like a mistake, the centre-half's thigh would propel the ball back into the opposition half. No-one ever seemed to read what was going to happen and the trick worked again and again. The other aspect in which he was different lay in his ability to organise those around him. They could see the game from their point of view. He saw it from a team viewpoint.

Oh . . . his name? Jock Stein.

The same man who became a legend in Scotland by managing Celtic to the first success by a British team in the European Cup and who led them to nine successive Scottish First Division title before, sadly, dying on the touchline in Wales where he was managing Scotland.

Jock was not the only interesting football character I got to know well. Playing in the same Celtic team was a left winger (this was the days when it was easy to describe a player's position on the field and before the stupid tags that are given today) called Charles Patrick Tully.

Now Charlie would never head a ball, he was relatively slow, he would never tackle and his physique left a lot to be desired – signs of a pot belly in his 20's was an example. However, he was a master with the ball. He would bear down on a defender, seem to do nothing, but leave the poor confused bloke wondering how he got goal-side. Then he would deliver a perfect cross for someone like Billy McPhail, a master in the air, to nod into the net. He also scored goals from corners – by memory he was credited with two such in a game at Falkirk. The first one was ruled out by the referee, so he promptly did the same from the second and it was allowed.

His problem, like so many geniuses with a ball, was that between games he liked 'a wee dram' which sounded very innocent in his Irish accent, but was anything but. Being that I worked for a spell as sports editor of the Irish edition of *The Weekly News* we got on well and I recall even this far away deciding to have a chat with him and calling on his home on the south side of Glasgow. No mansions then with security gates and an assortment of top of the range cars in the drive, but a simple semi-detached house like so many all over the country.

There was a rambling rose on the outside wall and it had rambled uncontrolled so much that it was like a sentinel across the front door. Pushing it aside, I knocked and while I was waiting, looked down and saw several pint bottles of milk on the doorstep. At first I thought, 'He's gone and forgotten to stop the milk delivery,' but as I was turning away there was sound from inside the house, so I waited. After what seemed an age, the door was unlocked and slowly opened. The sight that greeted me was one of 'how not to look in the morning' or any other time for that matter. It was Charlie, receding hair all over the place with more head than hair showing, an old shirt almost half off his body and a pair of trousers that were even more crumpled than the face above them. Gradually he focused and recognised me.

"Could you come back later, Ian?" he asked.

I readily agreed as it was obviously no time to be talking business!

Watching a Raith Rovers reserve game when in Kirkcaldy one wet, miserable winter day I found myself gradually being absorbed in a superb display of skill from a slim, dark-haired youngster at left-half. He seemed to be almost exclusively left-footed, but his control of the ball meant that didn't make any difference to his ability to beat opponents and deliver passes measured to an inch.

I inquired about him, wrote a small piece. That was my first, indirect, contact with the football genius that was Jim Baxter. Hardly had the ink dried on my piece than rumour had it that Jim was on his way to Glasgow Rangers. And so it turned out.

By this time I had my own 'howff' (meeting place) in Glasgow – the cafe in Renfield Street owned by the Rangers great George Young and Rangers goalkeeper George Niven. On any given week you could have chosen a top class Scotland team from the players I met and interviewed there, usually while eating Lorne (Square) sausage, chips and beans. The Jamie Oliver's of today would have an attack of the vapours over the food, but it was fresh, the place was clean and the football chat that swirled around, priceless. On this particular day I was making inroads into my Lorne when a voice with a very distinct Fife accent said,

"You Ian Wheeler?" I looked up and immediately recognised young Baxter.

"Yes," I replied, "what can I do for you?"

"You wrote a bit about me in *The People's Journal* didn't you?" he said.

Anticipating – as a journalist mostly does – verbal blast of criticism, I replied, "Indeed I did."

"Then I'll tell you this," he said, by this time sitting opposite me, "that was the first time anybody wrote anything about me. They'll write a lot more yet and if ever you want a story you have only to give me a shout and you'll get it."

After I had mentally returned from a defensive feeling, I asked him, big deal, if he fancied a meal.

"No," he said, "but you can tell me where I can buy a rain coat. It's always bloody raining in Glasgow and I haven't got one."

"No problem," I answered, "easiest way is to go to Lewis's polytechnic (a huge store in Argyle Street) and take your pick."

So we duly did just that, Jim buying the first one he tried on. Next day I was again in the cafe, this time interviewing a Hearts player who lived in Glasgow when a familiar voice said, "Ian . . . you got a minute?" It was Jim and after I had finished my chat with the other player I joined him. What was the problem?

"Could you take me back to that place for a coat? I lost mine," he said. And that was when I realised this genius with a football maybe had flaws! This particular flaw was an all-night party, then straight into training at Ibrox, where he had left his coat "after a few drinks" to quote him, "and I can't remember where the hell the party was."

So back we went to Lewis's, where Jim bought another coat (which he didn't lose for three days). Not long after this, meeting old friend Bob Shankly in the hotel where his Dundee team gathered before a game against Rangers that very day, Bob asked me to follow him. We went along a corridor and in the alcove at the end of it was Jim Baxter – and a rum and coke in the glass in front of him. How do I know? He told me and Bob what it was and that it was "my favourite drink."

Superb as a player, his performance against England at Wembley the year after the Auld Enemy won the World Cup was sheer class and arrogance. His week in week out ability for Rangers, in what I consider the classiest Ibrox team I have ever seen – Niven, Shearer, Cladow, Davis, Paterson, Baxter, Scott (later Henderson), McMillan, Millar, Brand and Wilson – was made 'tick' by him and his on-field partner Ian McMillan. But oh, that demon drink! So young, so talented, so flawed, so likeable, and so dead too early.

Briefly there I mentioned another great character, Willie Henderson. When the flying winger Alex Scott left Rangers for Everton and further deserved success there was a feeling among the Rangers support that he would never be replaced. But waiting in the wings – literally – was a 5ft 4ins star who at least equalled the Scott influence and at times might even have surpassed it.

I first saw wee Willie, as he was known by the Rangers support, playing for Greengairs School in a game at Airdrie's then home, Broomfield Park. On the invitation of Airdrie chairman Mr Peter Bennie, a former school headmaster with an undying love of football, I went to the game to see 'someone who will definitely become a star.'

Lanarkshire schoolboy teams of that era had many players who went on to successful careers in professional football, so I didn't know who exactly I would be seeing with the most star potential. It took me all of five minutes to be in no doubt. This stocky little lad on the left wing went past defenders as if they weren't there, scored two himself and laid on three more in next to no time. At the end of the game I didn't need to say "I saw who you mean" to Mr Bennie, but I did anyway.

"Yes," said the chairman, "and we would love to have him here, but he is too good a player and will be on a big club's books very soon."

And he was spot on again, with Willie joining Rangers as a teenager. We became firm friends and he was a regular visitor to 'my' howff for a lunch and a chat. At which point I came across an amazing fact about the player who could pinpoint a cross ball to within inches, and could dazzle defenders with his footwork. It happened one day when we were leaving the cafe together.

"I'm getting the bus," said Willie, so I stood at the bus stop with him.

There were several busses which picked up and let down at the stop and as the first one slowed a matter of feet away, I was asked, "What number is that?" Having normal eyesight I had noted the number quite a distance away, Willie couldn't see it even when it stopped. He was virtually blind, or so short-sighted it was ridiculous considering what he did on the football field.

Glasgow had given me much of what I wanted in sports journalism but there was a big flaw. First though, the important things. A game which will never be forgotten and a friendship which I cherished.

Among the hundreds of games I reported on over my career, ranging from Highland League all the way to the pinnacle of four World Cup tournaments, one stood out in isolation – at the very top of the tree.

It was Real Madrid v Eintracht Frankfurt in the final of the European Cup at Hampden Park in 1960.

I had stood on the terraces of the old Hampden to watch several Scotland games – once with my new wife, when the crowd was 138,000, and she ruined a pair of shoes in the mud. She was only saved from pitching forward on her face as the crowd swayed by a Birmingham City fan who grabbed about an inch of her coat and somehow kept her upright. There were no seats on the terracing in 1948, or for a long time afterwards and though there were crush barriers, they were dangerous in themselves because if you were forced against them, as my father once was, you could seriously damage your ribs.

How was it an Englishman who saved her? Because you could stand among opposition supporters in those days and I had got my tickets from an English source to enjoy the banter of being set upon as an enemy.

But, back to that final. Real stood alone at the pinnacle of world football, with truly great players of the calibre of Alfredo di Stefano, Ferenc Puskas and Gento in the forward line and other stars all over the place. I had the added privilege, prior to the game, of being allowed to join the team and officials for an evening; then a morning training session. Today, sports writers have to attend press conferences and be 'handed' someone to interview, with managers allowing only those they think will say little or nothing important. If the questioning gets a bit intense, the player's agent will be on the phone in an instant trying to get payment for what he claims is an 'exclusive' – an 'exclusive' which appears in at least half-a-dozen newspapers, television and radio, not to mention mobile phones and computers.

Changed days indeed – then I was allowed to sit with the greatest players in the world and chat through an interpreter; no supervision, no discussion about what questions I asked, in short, no interference of any kind. And I got my stories for *The Weekly News,* with two abiding memories above all others; the amount of wine consumed during the evening, regardless of a final being 48 hours away and the quote from the great Sefano to the effect that he did not believe in heading the ball, that football was played on the ground.

This led to a classic heading from sports editor John Rankine –"'Ze 'ead is for wearing ze' at," says di Stefano. Johnny never cringed but he must have come close when he read that in later years!

The training session was a revelation in more ways than one. First a pompous Willie Waddell, a Rangers and Scotland right wing legend, then managing Kilmarnock, tried to stop me entering Rugby Park to watch the Real training session.

"I decide who enters this stadium," he claimed. Before I could retort, I was nudged aside by an interpreter who informed him that on this occasion at least he was wrong, that in fact the gentleman standing just behind us approved of Mr Wheeler watching the training. I turned to find that gentleman was Senor Bernebau, the man who created the club that was Real and who has the Madrid stadium named after him because of what he did for the club. I thanked him and he smiled and indicated that I should go ahead into the ground.

Somehow, Waddell and I never got on after that – and when he turned to writing a column for a daily newspaper I saw him excluded from the Press bus on a Scotland trip to Switzerland because of the way he had treated football writers when managing both Kilmarnock and Rangers. I voted for the exclusion and that vote was unanimous.

And the training session? The players knocked the ball about, Gento performed a few tricks like stepping over the ball, flicking it over his head with his heel and racing – and he really could race – on to it as it landed ahead of him, then they trooped back on to the bus to return to their hotel. Anti-climax? I'll say!

So much has been written about the game itself – which Real won 7-3 against a team that would probably have beaten any other in Europe at the time – that I don't need to go into details. But I do have another abiding memory connected to the event. Beside me in the Press box was a Spanish journalist, about 5ft 7ins tall and eight stones soaking wet.

As hysteria about the game deservedly increased, the roars from the largely Scottish crowd of 130,000 swept across the stadium and a fair piece of Glasgow, too. My Spanish pal could hardly contain himself, "You wonderful people," . . . "Scottish is the greatest." . . . the praise for the hordes on the terracing and in the grandstands grew and grew. After the post-match interviews and with things winding down, we met again.

"Could I give you a lift back to town," I asked. He accepted. I took him to the Central Hotel in the heart of the city and there he shared a drink with my London colleague, Charlie Holloway. I stayed for the chat only as I was driving and they toasted Real, then Bernebau, then di Stefano, then Puskas, then Gento, then Eintracht, then the crowd, then Scotland, then . . . well, you get the gist. Before I left I helped both of them to their respective rooms, the little Spaniard being carried, Charlie managing to steer his own course – just! Yes, unforgettable and not just for the greatest club game I ever saw out of the thousands all over the world.

The other abiding memory of Scotland 1953-63 was of meeting and becoming friendly with the man I rate alongside Alf Ramsey, Jock Stein, Matt Busby, Bill Shankly, Bob Paisley, Brian Clough and one or two others as the best in the business.

His name BOB Shankly, brother of Bill and compared to his brother, virtually unknown. I first met him when I had to go to Falkirk to cover a game for the *Sunday Post*. There were no Press conferences after a game in those days, but I bumped in to him as I was leaving after writing my report and introduced myself. We ended up chatting about the game and he must have felt I had got it right because he said if I needed a Falkirk story I should 'nip down from Glasgow' for a chat in mid-week.

Because any reporting job is about having good contacts in the business involved, I did just that the next week and for almost every week thereafter. I probably learned more about the game and the people in it from this man than from anyone else since my original mentor back in Elgin, Willie Robertson. Bob produced a team at Falkirk that was the envy of just about every other manager in Scotland. Then he moved to Third Lanark and did the same again.

My regular visits continued, sitting in his tiny Cathkin Park office in the all-wooden stand that frequently went on fire because of people (sometimes reporters) dropping their cigarette butts through the gaps in the floor of the stand on match days. And we talked, as always, football, football and more football – until one grey, rainy, typically Glasgow day when he said he wanted to ask me something and would only chat out in the middle of the pitch.

As we stood there getting steadily soaked he said, "You worked in Dundee, you know the place and the people and you have contacts with the Dens Park (Dundee) club. Could you get me information on the club, the directors, the players and the rest? I know a lot of it, but you might find out something that I don't know?"

I asked the obvious question "Why?"

"Because they have approached me to be their manager – and if you breathe a word of that we're finished as friends," he said.

A journalist is never supposed to turn down a story, but there are exceptions, as in this case where I was guaranteed many in the future for holding back on one. In other words I had a 'scoop' on my hands but didn't use it – in favour of an 'investment' which proved over the years that followed to be the correct decision . . . and Bob's name was already being mentioned as Dundee manager among many others!

So I got him his information; he weighed up everything and moved to Dundee, which was the best move that club ever made. Historically he won the club their first ever league title in 1961-62, reached the semi-final of the European Cup the next season and introduced to the game several players who are among the best 'home products' ever to grace a football ground.

Pat Liney was an unheralded, but extremely efficient goalkeeper, Alex Hamilton and Bobby Cox were as good a pair of full backs as I have seen at club level. Ian Ure, a blonde giant, was a rock at centre-half and inside forwards Andy Penman and Alan Cousin, though entirely different in style and approach – Cousin long-striding with a deceptive 'double shuffle' in his armoury, Penman wise about the game beyond his years – had a perfect understanding. Out on the left there was the trickery of Hugh Robertson and crowning it all, at centre-forward, Alan Gilzean. Few have ever even equalled his heading skills and ability to be in exactly the right place at the right time to score goals. He is immortalised in Dundee and achieved the same status with Tottenham Hotspur.

A young team, "Too young," manager Shankly told me within weeks of his appointment. So he added exactly the right quota of experience into the side. Wing-halves (now they would be dully called midfielders) Bobby Seith and Bobby Wishart had enjoyed success with Burnley and Aberdeen respectively and Gordon Smith, a winger of true class, who had graced the right wing with Hibernian's Famous Five of Smith, Johnstone, Reilly, Turnbull and Ormond. The latter was considered by Hibs as past his best, and was snapped up for Dundee.

The mix was 100 per cent correct. Bob Shankly had master-minded possibly the best and definitely the most successful Dundee team ever. Only the best win the top league and they and they alone have done it in Dundee's history.

The subtleties introduced by the experienced Seith, Wishart and Smith perfectly blended with the enthusiasm and skill of the young players and a new Dundee F.C. was born and flourished. But, in time, even success has its drawbacks.

"We have too many good young players in too many positions," the manager confided to me in a private conversation after a game in which they had outclassed Glasgow Rangers. "Compared to some we are a small club and we will never keep all these lads."

Again he was right. There were constant attempts to sign Hamilton, the bubbly, outgoing attacking full back (probably the first of his kind) and Cox, one of the best tacklers I have ever seen, which were resisted, but Ure went to Arsenal, Glizean to Spurs and Penman to Rangers. With Smith ageing and replacements never quite matching the standard of those who left, it was a downward spiral.

The fact remains that Bob Shankly cemented his position as a truly outstanding manager and definitely deserves at least equal credit as his brother Bill, who pulled an ailing Liverpool F.C. together and created a power in the game that lasts to this day.

Chapter Eight

Leaving Glasgow and Moving On

Though I had everything in place in Glasgow and in Scottish football, I was becoming restless. Frankly the constant Catholic-Protestant thing which ruled the city and its football was getting to me. One Rangers fan – who still owes me, nearly 50 years on for a handful of Scotland-England tickets! – was the perfect example. I was chatting with Billy McNeil, later to captain Celtic to European Cup glory, and Pat Crerand, who a year later won the same trophy with Manchester United, outside Celtic Park before a game.

On the following Monday the Rangers fanatic came at me in the street with "What were you doing speaking to these bastards McNeil and Crerand on Saturday?"

"My job," I answered. Then tried him with, "and how do you know where I was and who I was speaking to?"

"Because a mate dropped me there after a job and I was spitting on the pavement outside that dump before I saw you," was the sick answer.

And suddenly there was an opportunity to move on. A Glasgow colleague, John Dunn, had gone to Newcastle-upon-Tyne to cover for all D C Thomson newspapers a couple of years earlier, but had suddenly decided to decamp to the *Sunday Express*.

"That job open?" I asked Glasgow editorial chief Sandy Reid.

"Yes . . . you interested?" he answered.

Having discussed the possibility with my wife I said "Yes."

Within a week the move had been confirmed and within another couple of days I was on my way south; possibly the beginning of the most important move of my working life. But it didn't start that way. It was early 1963 and the weather was awful. Heavy snowfalls and freezing temperatures had made the roads like ski runs and I was driving south to Carlisle then turning left for Newcastle in a not-too-new Morris 1000. At Beattock summit I pulled into a lay-by, shattered.

I had to get to my destination though, and after a half-hour rest I was off again, sliding and slithering along at about an average 15-20 miles an hour, which was taking chances, but had to be done. Eventually, after ten hours of possibly the worst drive of my life I made it to my destination – the Corner House Hotel in Newcastle. I went to bed at 8 that night after my one meal of the day (I still recall their marvellous and huge roast potatoes) and slept like a log until eight next morning. Even then I was still tired, but at least I was where I wanted to be.

Things didn't get much better for quite a time. First of all there was a huge backlog of work to tackle, then, when I went to view the semi-detached house in Killingworth station which was to be our family home, I found that our neighbours were extremely stand-offish and strangely reluctant to have any conversation. It was only when my wife and family joined me and we actually occupied the house that we found why.

John Dunn had told them to be careful of us, that I had come as a 'hatchet man' to take over his (?) job. Nothing could have been further from the truth. He had moved on and I had been sent to replace him. We were also a happy and outgoing family who never failed to make friends. It took us a few weeks and a couple of 'getting to know you' parties before it was all sorted out and the truth emerged. From then on we settled in perfectly, especially with next door neighbours, John and Nan Batey and across the road Jed and Sheila Yellowlee.

This applied particularly to my family, wife Mildred, daughter Laura and son Graeme, because it was our first ever real house after 13 years of marriage and they revelled in that. The children had rooms to themselves and a front and back garden to play in. Perfect. On the bus one day Mildred heard a young Newcastle lass say of our children "They speak like Fancie and Josie mam" (a Scots duo – Rikkie Fulton and Jack Milroy – who were all the rage on television at the time, so it was said in admiration not criticism and did them no harm.)

But first there was work. There were around 40 'customers complaints' to be answered, where readers wrote in about work done, or not done by firms and asked the *Sunday Post* to help. Also backlogged was over 100 'Can I help' items, where readers wrote in asking for help in finding something they couldn't trace themselves.

It was a huge task to sort out that lot, but with tremendous help from my wife, who more or less cleared the Can I Help queries on her own, we got through it in the amazing short time of eight weeks, leaving us clear to catch up with more recent queries on both issues. I was then able to concentrate more and more on filling the north-east sports pages of *The Weekly News,* reporting on north-east games for *The Sunday Post* and being available for any work for our other papers. Not that this was easy because for the first six weeks there was no football! The snow that had hindered my arrival was still around and had built into huge drifts all over the area – in Consett, for instance, it was so deep only the top couple of feet of telephone poles were showing, the rest out of sight in the snow.

So no games. No stories? No. I had the good fortune to know a lot of Scots players in the area; Dave Hilley, Gordon Marshall, Willie Penman, with Newcastle United; George Mulhall and Nick Sharkey at Sunderland; George McGeachie at Middlesbrough and Scots I didn't know but who were soon to become friends at Hartlepool, Darlington and so on. Without their backing I would have been in trouble, but they talked to me, introduced me to their team-mates and generally made it possible for me to fill the appropriate pages.

I had another advantage. Back in Elgin there was the big Royal Engineers camp during the war and serving there was a young footballer called Joe Harvey. I had interviewed him and wrote a piece about him for my first newspaper. I kept tabs on him when he captained Newcastle United to FA Cup success twice, before he eventually became manager of the club. I phoned him for an appointment shortly after my arrival and turned up at his office a lunch time one Monday.

When I introduced myself, his first words were, "I think we've met before," and when I explained where and when, I was accepted right away – not always the case in football when a new reporter turns up! So even when there were no games my page had a fair share of Newcastle stories.

Sunderland manager was Alan Brown, a hard taskmaster who had done wonders at Burnley and came close to doing the same for the Wearside club, but didn't quite make it. An early heated 'debate' with Alan resulted in him saying, "If you had said that to me not long ago I'd have thrown you out of the office," to which I replied that it would have been a good fight. It wouldn't have been – he was a lot tougher and fitter than me, but I knew that he had by then turned to a religious outlook on life which didn't include violence.

Alan also gave me one of the best quotes I ever had from a manager. I was doing a version of his life story for *The Weekly News* and one of my questions to him was, "You've had your ups and downs as a player and manager. What is the worst thing that could happen as a manager?" After the briefest of pauses, he gave me his reply :

"To win everything available; the European Cup, the First Division (the Premier League of the day), the League Cup and the F.A. Cup – in one season."

After digesting this unique, and certainly unexpected answer, I came back with, "But surely that's the best thing, not the worst?"

"Think so?" He said. "What if you missed out on even one of those the following season? The club directors and, even more so, the supporters, would crucify you. Best thing to do after success like that would be to resign and take up gardening or something."

Was he correct? Most managers would chance winning everything and take it from there; but that was Alan, different to say the least.

Further south in my area was Middlesbrough F.C. Here, the manager was Raich Carter. His hair had turned grey early in his life and when he starred for Derby County and England he was referred to as 'the silver-haired maestro'. It was a fitting description as I had witnessed him play in the famous Derby team alongside Stamps and (Peter) Doherty while serving in the Fleet Air Arm. His only problem was that, like too many ex-players who move on to the manager's chair, he dwelt too much on reminiscences about his playing career rather than using it to teach current players about the game. He also had alongside him the vast experience of Harold Shepherdson, rated so highly that he became a key member of Alf Ramsey's off-field team which, a few years later, was instrumental in helping England win the World Cup.

However, the combination didn't bring success to 'Boro and I have always looked on them as the least effective of the north-east's major teams – even though Newcastle and Sunderland have under-achieved more often than not.

Working in Dundee I had been used to watching a successful team in the Billy Steel inspired Dundee F.C. In Glasgow, Rangers in the era of Jim Baxter and Ian McMillan, Shearer, Caldow, Davis, Paterson, Scott, Henderson, Millar Brand and Wilson, and Hearts inspired by Alex Young and Dave Mackay (later of Everton and Tottenham Hotspur respectively) and including, Marshall, Kirk, Mackenzie Milne, Cumming, Rutherford, Murray, Wardhaugh and Hamilton had produced great performances. But here, in the north-east, it was a case of under-achievement. Newcastle weren't helped by a running feud between two directors, ex-player Stan Seymour and lawyer Alderman McKeag.

What one said, the other contradicted. What one wanted the other knocked-back. I recall an interview with Seymour in which he said many things about the direction in which the club was going. The ink had scarcely dried on the Weekly News article when there was a phone call from McKeag threatening all sorts of retribution on me, Seymour, The Weekly News, the editor . . . and just about everyone else he could think of.

When he had finished, I said, "There's an easy solution. Put all you are saying into words in an interview and it will appear on the same page in the same paper and at the same length in the next issue."

After a splutter or two, he said he would get back to me. And he did. He gave the interview and it appeared exactly as promised because I was lucky enough to get the editor to agree. I heard no more on the issue, except from a close friend of McKeag's. It appeared that he not only read the article – he also counted the number of lines it occupied. Hearing this, I also counted. It was actually a few lines shorter, but he obviously had had enough.

Sunderland did come near to promotion one season. They had a top class team with Jimmy Montgomery in goal, an excellent half-back line of Martin Harvey (Northern Ireland), skipper Charlie Hurley (Republic of Ireland) and Jimmy McNab (Scotland) and forwards of the calibre of Scot George Herd and Irishman Johnny Crossan. They got to the last game of the season and faced Chelsea, managed at the time by a good friend of mine, Tommy Docherty, an outstanding wing-half with Preston North End and Scotland, and a man who epitomised the quick-fire, one line humour of the native Glaswegian.

Tommy was to become noted as the 'man with more clubs than Jack Nicklaus' but don't let that take away from the fact that he really was as good off the field as he had been on it. The fact that so many clubs used his ability is proof of that – and they don't come much bigger than Chelsea and later, Manchester United.

At this time it was Chelsea. The game was tense but, unlike so many in the play-off situations, full of good football. So was it decided by a piece of wizardry, of genius, of high level skill? Well, not quite! The vital goal was scored for Chelsea, by Tommy Harmer who was in fact the smallest and lightest player on the park. To call it a scrambled affair is to flatter it. The ball actually bounced in off a part of his anatomy that meant he had to have treatment from the club physiotherapist before he could celebrate.

Asked afterwards for his comment on so vital a goal, even manager Docherty, the man of a million words and ready quips, paused lengthily before saying, "The best I can do is say he actually made a balls of it."

I left Roker Park, Sunderland's ground at the time, over two hours after the end of the game, having witnessed an amazing mix of jubilation and depression. Outside a red-and-white scarfed Sunderland supporter was slumped against the wall of the stand, crying. I probably should have interviewed him, but there was a rule in journalism then that you didn't intrude on private grief and, believe me, this was private grief.

It has often been said that had Brian Clough, who averaged a goal a game with Sunderland, not been unavailable because of the knee ligament injury that finished his career, Sunderland would have won the game and promotion. That is impossible to prove one way or the other. A small, stocky Scot, Nick Sharkey, who had taken his place was a good player, had a good game, but was in the impossible position suffered by so many in that he was being asked to follow a legend – a situation which has cost many a player dearly.

Speaking about Clough. I had met him – and immediately fallen out with him. On one Sunderland visit and after chatting with the manager, I went down to the boot room to see who was around and before I got there I could hear a raised voice. It turned out to be Clough having a verbal go at an old retainer who was cleaning boots. He had to stop as he was suffering a nose bleed, but Clough carried on. I took the old boy's side and while he went away for treatment Clough and I had a shouting match. Gradually though, we cooled and eventually chatted quite amicably, which was to stand me in good stead when he became one of the great managers in the game in England.

One of his little habits intrigued me. Though I was a good ten years older than him, he always referred to me as 'young man.' If we hadn't met for a while his greeting would be, "Hello, young man. Good to see you."

I asked him once why he used the phrase. In typical Clough fashion his answer was, "D'you know how many people want to speak to me, young man? I can't remember every name, so . . . understand Ian?"

That was better than Billy McNeil, who captained Celtic to European Cup glory in 1967. I knew Billy from the time he was a new signing and worked in the office of legendary Celtic chairman, Bob Kelly. No matter where we met, no matter that he knew my name, no matter how famous he became the greeting was always the same – "Hello feyther (father)." Was that his Catholic upbringing, or for the same reason as Clough? I should have asked, but didn't.

* * *

Though I didn't realise it at the time, our stay in the north east was to be short, just under two years in fact. That said we are still delighted it happened. A real house for the family, a football daft area for me, wonderful friendly folk on Tyneside, Wearside and Teeside. People who have never been there seem to have a vision of pit bings (huge hills of waste from the coal mines) dull weather and dull people. Nothing could be further from the truth. If you want beautiful scenery and a lively lifestyle, it is one of the best places to be in Britain.

We had parties in our house, we went to parties in other houses and down from Glasgow came friends of Newcastle player and native Glaswegian Dave Hilley to entertain. We would go to a Working Men's Club and our star singer who had the build of a flyweight, wore glasses and had many spaces where his teeth should have been, would be introduced by Glasgow compere, Maxie who was magic with words and had the jokey approach of a star comedian.

The singer's favourite was The Hawaiian Wedding Song . . . and, as the song developed, tears flowed in the audience. I have heard the song sung many times though I have never heard it sung even half as well or with such emotion. At first there was a small crowd in the club, when he returned with the Glasgow lads the place was crowded. When I hear the rubbish produced by some of today's 'star' singers, I wonder why he didn't become a professional. Maybe he didn't look the part but his voice conquered any frailties.

I also managed a game of cricket, my first love as a player, while in the north east. It was a benefit match for the professional at Ashington and a motley crew of footballers, journalists and others faced the local team. Before the start we had what could be called 'a few jars'. Allowing that 'a few jars' of Newcastle Brown ale was to drinking what the hydrogen bomb was to destruction, it was a very relaxed team which took the field. I had been captain of our newspaper team in Glasgow. Prior to that I had started a cricket league in Elgin and played for a marvellous club called Norwood, in Dundee.

So I was no novice – but this game turned out to be a total personal disaster. Captain was a local newspaper sports writer to whom I never warmed and the feeling was mutual. So in I went around the middle order – and was bowled for a duck. With an ill-advised air of confidence, I took my turn as a bowler – slow, right arm, off spin. Was it coincidence that I went on at the end where I was downside of the slope on the pitch, which meant the spin was nullified and the ball kept going straight on? Whatever, the professional hit me for six fours in my only over!

Mind you, things weren't all bad. We adjourned to the club bar when the game was over and I hit the jackpot on the fruit machine for a total of £66, no mean win in 1964, especially in a club where the drink was cheaper than in a normal pub. Over to the bar I toddled, laid the lot on the counter and said, "Keep them coming as long as that lasts."

It was a hazy return to Newcastle and when we got there three or four wives were waiting having had to look after the children from early in the day to nearly midnight. They were not pleased and several marriages rocked on their foundations for a few days.

Oh yes, Newcastle certainly threw up memories!

Chapter Nine

Manchester Correspondent

With my time in the north-east almost over, again my next move was because of a colleague leaving. My first hint of it came from a journalist pal who asked me if I had heard that Len Noad, from our Manchester office, was leaving to join *The Sun* newspaper. I hadn't, but did very shortly after, when Noad telephoned me to ask if I fancied becoming The Sun sports writer in the north-east. He had the authority of an old Glasgow adversary Jimmy Stevenson, now northern sports editor of *The Sun*, to ask me. It isn't easy making a decision when a major daily comes on the scene, but after weighing it up carefully and discussing it with my wife, I said, "Thanks, but no thanks." What must be remembered at this stage was that it was a simple question of stay or go. Nothing else was on offer.

Yes, I would have earned more money, but not all that much allowing for tax and I would have had to find a house. Because I had moved around we were occupying one owned by the firm. So another attempt by a former colleague to say later that I moved into his (?) job was a lie. When I was contacted by our Dundee head office to discuss the possibility of filling the gap left by Noad moving on, it was the first I had heard of the idea.

I should have guessed? Maybe, but there were several others in various offices who could have been considered. It took us a much shorter time to decide on moving from the north-east to north-west England that I had to turn down *The Sun* offer.

We would have to leave a house we had loved, but we were moving to another in what was then an attractive Manchester suburb, Chorlton-cum-Hardy. I had settled into my job in a wonderful corner of England but, in a football sense, I would be moving to an even bigger arena.

The children? We checked and found their schooling would carry on as normal. So everything added up and we moved again yet once more things weren't simple. When we got to the house, the electrical wiring for all the lights had been cut back into the ceilings and walls, a metal gate had been handed over to neighbours, and the same tales as in Newcastle about me and us as a family had been spread around.

On one side of our new home we had a headmaster and family, on the other a policeman and family. Mr & Mrs Francis and son Peter soon became friends so it was only after the settling in period that I looked around, sat down to consider my new job and realised I had landed in a football writer's dream world.

I had made a point when in Glasgow and Newcastle of introducing myself to every English manager I came across, whether they were in Scotland on scouting missions, as they did every spring, or on other occasions. There was talent aplenty in teams north of the border. I also kept in touch with players I knew in those visiting outfits, renewing acquaintanceships with such as Dave Mackay, Danny Blanchflower, Cliff Jones and Bill Brown at Spurs; Alex Young, Alex Parker and Sandy Brown, Everton; Ron Yeats, Billy Stevenson and Ian St John, Liverpool; Jimmy McEwan, Aston villa; Denis Law, Manchester United; Wolves and England captain Billy Wright and many others.

I knew managers like Matt Busby, the creator of the giant that is now Manchester United; Bill Shankly; Don Revie, who created the best team Leeds United have ever had; Brian Clough, moving up the ranks from managing Hartlepool to inspiring Derby County then becoming immortalised in football with his creation of European giants in Nottingham Forest; Harry Catterick, who gave Everton League championship and FA up success; Bill Nicholson, the Yorkshireman who blended Spurs into a team admired everywhere; the inimitable Joe Mercer, captain of Arsenal and England as a player, manager of Sheffield United and Aston Villa, before in tandem with coach extraordinary, Malcolm Allison, doing a Phoenix with Manchester City. Above all, Alf Ramsey, the man who gave England its one and only World Cup success in 1966.

I was asked recently by a youngish football writer how it was that in a relatively short 14 seasons in England I knew and drew stories and articles from so many people. That was my answer. What he hadn't allowed for was years of hard work and building of contacts – the 'life blood' of any journalist – before I arrived in Manchester. It might all have meant little, but here I was in that city, bang in the centre of the area which had what I consider the greatest collection of outstanding managerial and player talent of all time.

I loved it. It was the realisation of a dream I'd had since I was a young lad back in Elgin, struggling to become a reporter and enjoying reading the way *The Weekly News* presented stories of and from personalities in Britain's major sport. Now I was with that very newspaper, which circulated some one million copies a week in England alone and many more in Scotland and Ireland.

But I had to produce the goods as well as being happy at my good fortune, and without being arrogant, I believe I did. I had been taught to think about the subject I was involved in as a reporter, to look for things of interest and to build questions. That teaching paid off and I thank all who helped, from Miss Robertson in Elgin onwards.

* * *

The question is where to start with recollections of a golden era in English football. Maybe with Matt, later Sir Matt Busby. I had met Matt checking out players in Scotland and when he was, briefly, manager of Scotland in a part-time capacity before the ghastly Munich air disaster which destroyed his team of all the talents.

Not long before Munich, I had also met the great Duncan Edwards, possibly destined to be the best English born player ever, though we will never know and can only speculate after watching the phenomenal maturity he displayed when little more than a boy. He played against Scotland in an under-23 game at Clyde's home ground at the time, Shawfield. Watching reporters could only look on in awe as he controlled the midfield with an ease above and beyond any expectations – then he moved to centre-forward because of injury and looked just as at home there. He died as a result of Munich, as did so many of his team-mates.

Also lost was England goalkeeper extraordinary turned reporter Frank Swift. Frank had entertained the Scottish Press corps attending a game in Liverpool to a night out at a local club and was the perfect host. He regaled us with stories including the one where Scotland's Billy Houliston, of Queen of the South, charged into him and broke his rib in an England-Scotland fixture at Wembley. Typically, he made fun of it.

To say we had a few drinks is a massive understatement. In fact we younger members of the corps had to carry one or two senior members to the train taking us back to Scotland – and we weren't all that 'fit' ourselves. Then, to crown all, when we slumped into our seats it was to be told that Craig Gordon of the SFA, had brought in a CRATE of whisky for the journey north. All I will add is that it had all gone before we staggered out of the train in Glasgow's Central station.

But back to Matt Busby. I had of course, visited the bomb site that was Old Trafford when I was in the Fleet Air Arm. It is almost unbelievable that it was the forerunner of the magnificent edifice that is there today. On my first visit in my new job, I recalled my visit to Matt and mentioned seeing a wooden hut outside the ground.

Matt immediately stopped me. "And if you had knocked on the door of that hut I would have come out to meet you," he said. "That was my office. We played at Maine Road (Manchester City's ground) but I kept that office at Old Trafford because I had to be on hand when the re-building was going on."

It was the start of a contact which was 90 per cent friendly over the years before I moved back north. I say 90 per cent because if a football writer is doing his job it is inevitable that he will clash with a club manager at some point – and Matt and I did, over George Best.

George and I got on well together. I knew him from the time he started becoming an idol to millions, until the days when he became an alcoholic. Finding him in his hey-day was a more than slightly difficult task. He should have been in his digs, at Mrs Fullarton's, or in the home he built for himself, but seldom was. With his drinking pals or, a beautiful girl? It was usually one or the other and it often wasn't anywhere in or around Manchester. He spread the net wide! It was in the days where, if you were trusted as a reporter, you could move reasonably freely around clubs.

I usually caught up with George, or Denis Law, Nobby Stiles, Pat Crerand and others either at their home or The Cliff, the old training ground. This day, though, I had a chat with George before a game, saw time was passing and said "I'll leave you to get ready." Half-an-hour later, at 2.40 (kick-off 3pm) I saw him again, chatting to a gorgeous young blonde girl in the foyer.

The next week, on a visit to manager Busby, I casually raised the question of whether all players had to report at the same time before a game.

"What are you getting at?" was the response.

"Nothing except that I saw George Best still in his normal clothes only 20 minutes before kick-off on Saturday," I said.

Matt exploded with a verbal blast I didn't know he was capable of. I was a sneak, I was undermining his club, I'd be banned . . . And these were the nicer things he said. At this point in his career George was getting really difficult to handle and it was obviously telling on his manager. I wasn't going to write the story, I had merely been making conversation because we were talking about how well Best had played in the game. Leaving behind a few comments of my own, I stormed out.

By the next day I was contemplating a ban by United and concentrating on the fact 'our' area contained 52 clubs from which I could get stories, interviews and so on. But just as I was getting ready to visit one or two of them, the phone rang. It was Matt. He wanted to see me. I switched my visit to take in Old Trafford and, sure enough, was ushered into his office. He didn't apologise, but merely said he had been a bit upset at the time and I wouldn't be banned. So things went back to normal, but I knew what Denis Law meant some time later when he told me Matt and he had fallen out on an issue about wages, "And I found out that he could be a lot less than Mr Nice Guy when you upset him."

Talking of Denis Law – one of the bubbliest characters in the game, as quick with a quip as he was on his feet when playing. Well, normally that is. His career with Manchester United was outstanding even by the standards of that huge club – a record £115,000 purchase from Torino, 237 goals in 439 games – but like all careers it had to end and when it did he stayed in his beloved adopted city of Manchester and signed for United greatest rivals, even including Liverpool, Manchester City.

City were on the up, United fading to well below their accepted standard; so much so that the seeming impossibility of relegation kept looming larger and larger. The fateful day duly arrived, with City the opposition and Law leading their attack. We should all have known the outcome beforehand, but perhaps even a fiction writer would have been laughed at for suggesting it. Though he was more than just a goal-scoring machine, Law had the knack of getting goals that were decisive – and none more decisive, in his mind, than this one.

The ball arrived when he had his back to goal. "My instinct clicked in," he told me not long after (he wouldn't speak in the immediate aftermath), "and I back-heeled it. It had hardly crossed the line when I thought, I've put United down. So I walked off and was substituted."

United would have been relegated anyway, but until this was pointed out to him Denis had,

" . . . the worst moments of my playing career. And even though I hadn't actually relegated United it still hurt me that it had happened."

The fact he had signed for City, never mind scored against United, still rankles with now elderly United followers, but it has to be remembered that the Law signing sequence was Huddersfield Town, MANCHESTER CITY, for £55,000, a record at the time; Torino, then United and City again. So really, his arrival in the twilight of his career was as much a bit of a homecoming as anything and lasted only a season.

Attacking players in the game, in any game for that matter, always attract more publicity than defenders, but that doesn't stop defenders being key figures – none more so than centre-half Bill Foulkes. A team-mate of Law's in the great years of the 1960's, he played in a total of 688 first team games in a 1950 to 1970 career. Big, tough and though he won only one cap for England, a close challenger to Jackie Charlton in the run-up to places in the 1966 World Cup winning team.

Bill was United's anchor in defence and his uncompromising play might have misled people into thinking he was as tough and hard off the field as on it . . . which would be wrong. Like so many who display an outward image he was in truth a most approachable person and one who thought deeply about things. He had been a hero of the Munich air disaster which decimated the United team in 1958. He and goalkeeper Harry Gregg had miraculously survived and were among those who bravely helped in the rescue attempts immediately following the crash.

It was now some nine years after the disaster and a new group of players, other than Munich survivors Foulkes and Bobby Charlton, had emerged and included Goalkeeper Alex Stepney, full backs Shay Brennan and Tony Dunne; midfielders Pat Crerand and Nobby Stiles; forwards George Best, Denis Law, David Herd, John Aston, defender or forward David Sadler and occasional others. Not only new, but successful because they won the First Division title for the first time in those nine years.

Last game of the season was against Stoke City, the title already won, but with 61,000 people inside Old Trafford, 99 per cent of them celebrating the fact. At the end of an easily forgettable 0-0 draw, the players stayed on the field to celebrate with the supporters, but from my Press box eyrie, I couldn't spot Bill Foulkes. Access to lower reaches of the stand on occasion wasn't denied me so I headed off for the home dressing room. I knocked on the door, heard "OK, come in" and when I did so I saw only Bill, in the bath on his own.

After the hellos and "well done" from me, I wondered out loud why he wasn't out on the field celebrating. "I'm as happy as the rest," was the reply, "but I thought my place was to be alone with my thoughts and memories of the lads who died in Munich. It's a great day but, for many of us, a sad one too." Tough, hard, yes on the field, but very human too. It wasn't the time for an interview. An intrusion into reflection time for someone entitled to his privacy despite the occasion, so I said "see you later," and left.

A year later, when United won the European Cup by beating Benfica 4-1 at Wembley, Best and Charlton were big in the headlines, but one round earlier Bill was the hero. In the semi-final he scored one of only nine goals he managed for United in his career – but what a goal. It was the winner against Real Madrid in the semi-final and propelled his team into the unforgettable event not long after.

I had the privilege of being a guest at the private after-match dinner following the final and reasoned that of all those deservedly celebrating victory, none deserved it more than Bill, Bobby Charlton and their manager Matt, soon to be Sir Matt Busby.

As the most progressive manager of his day he, along with Hibs in Scotland, had wanted to go into Europe and compete in the European trophies being built into various competitions. They eventually succeeded in their ambition, despite the opposition of die-hard 'who needs that, we are the big time not Europe?' and this was the successful culmination of his hard work and determination.

. . . and then there was another Scot – the one and only Bill Shankly.

Never in all my time in the game did I meet anyone who had such a rapport with the people who followed his team. Born in Ayrshire, Scotland, a successful player with Preston North End, coaching jobs at several clubs . . . then he 'came home'. No, not to Scotland, not to Preston but to Liverpool, a city with which he only previously had a fleeting contact. Immediately he was as one with anyone who was in any way connected to the Anfield club.

People talk about legends. He was the prime example. Maybe he didn't walk on water but the people who were in any way connected with Liverpool FC believed that he could. When he appeared to take his place in the Liverpool dug-out it was as if the Messiah had arrived.

He believed managing this club, which he pulled from relative obscurity to a position they have rightly held since his days in Britain, in Europe and the world of football, was his destiny, his calling. The crumbling edifice that had been Anfield was gradually transformed into an arena which visiting clubs, in the huge majority, visited with the deepest respect and in some cases, genuine fear. This was epitomised in the sign he insisted on having painted on a ledge, impossible to miss as the players took to the field.

It read 'This Is Anfield' and it carried the unwritten message that you were facing a task likely to be beyond you.

I remember the truly great England and West Ham team captain Bobby Moore telling me, "It shouldn't be any more than a sign to a visiting player, but it had a strange way of making you wonder if you were worthy of being there. Some of us shrugged off the idea, others didn't." Bobby himself? He wouldn't say, but I always felt he was never at this best at Anfield.

There were those who thought Shankly was just a fanatical football lover who made sure his players were fit and who could pick the right ones for various jobs on the field. In that they were correct, but they also underestimated by miles, his intelligence and ability to get into the minds of the opposition and his own players.

Long before modern managers were talking about 'player psychology', Shankly and his team of assistants Bob Paisley, Joe Fagan, Ronnie Moran and Roy Evans practiced on a constantly evolving group of players. Bob had a 'magic black box' secreted from Germany which had properties that had injured players believing it could deal with just about any injury in half the time normal methods took. Not really. It was the forerunner of the Tens machine, based on electrical impulses 'hitting' the central spot of an injury. Yes, it was an advance on a bit of massage and was well ahead of the cold sponge on-the-field treatment, but a whole lot of the recovery from injury was down to players believing it was getting them better faster.

" . . . and what about the injury?" I inquired which had been suffered by an international player who had an inclination to duck out of training on occasions with an unspecified back, leg, ankle or whatever knock? Normally Bill and I had a chat in his diminutive office under the main stand, but this time he hustled me out and we halted outside the treatment room.

"Ask me out loud about him again," he whispered.

So I did – and in full Shankly voice he answered, "We're really worried about him. He keeps getting knocks. There's a promising laddie in the reserves who could take over, but if that doesn't work we'll have to buy . . . and we know who that will be."

The whole chat was loud enough to be heard in and beyond the treatment room. I asked a few additional questions, none of them very important. Then he said, "Have to go now. See you next time you are over," and we went our separate ways (with me phoning later to ask who the 'replacement' might be and being told "don't be daft . . . ").

That 'injured' player suddenly became someone seen in the treatment room only on very few occasions – and held down a regular berth in the team for a few seasons. Psychology or what!

And the Shankly fund of one liners? Ad libs – or not. I wouldn't say he practiced them, but let's agree that they sometimes lacked a little . . . spontaneity!

Though the Shankly-Paisley partnership saw the rise of Liverpool Football Club to respect and admiration throughout the world of football, I felt that increasingly, there was tension between them. Bill was manager for 15 years and that, I believe, was too long in Bob's mind in that he felt he deserved a chance of the top job instead of being effectively No. 2. We were driving along Princes Street in Edinburgh, before a European Cup game against Hibernian when I first got the feeling of unrest on Bob's part. Bill gave the most amazing summary of Edinburgh's historic statues and monuments I have ever heard. It was a five-star guided tour and he interspersed it with one-liners.

Sitting with Bob, I said, "That's brilliant. He's a lot more than just a football man, obviously." The reply surprised me.

"It could all have come out of a book and probably did – and the one liners don't just happen, he rehearses them."

How true was this? Well I never actually saw Bill 'rehearsing ad libs', but he wasn't averse to borrowing them. The now legendary "Football isn't about life or death it's more important than that" came via a chat with a reporter. Talking about a game which Liverpool lost, the reporter said." . . . but it isn't a life or death thing, Bill." The reply was,

"No it's more important than that." This developed into "Football isn't etc . . . "

My own contribution to Shankly quotes came after a game against Bolton Wanderers. Liverpool had, surprisingly played badly in the first game, but survived to have a replay. This they won 5-1 by memory. Visiting Anfield next day I had my usual chat with Bill.

"At the game last night?" he asked – (there never was any game but the one Liverpool was involved in).

"Yes," I replied.

"Good, eh?"

"Yes . . . in fact it was men against boys." That quote come out of my memory bank and had been used by a Petty Officer about, of all things, a navy team which had easily won a tug-o'-war team competition.

"Ay," said Bill after a pause, "men against boys." "Aye."

That night he was interviewed on television about the replay. "You could say it was men against boys," he told the interviewer, who was so pleased with the reply he repeated it. So another Shankly quote (?) became legend.

However, among the many quotes rightly assigned to him, he did describe that marvellous giant of a centre-half Ron Yeats, signed from Dundee United as a 'Colossus', when walking round him and introducing him to photographers after the signing on ceremony and he did tell Jock Stein after Celtic had become the first British team to win the European Cup, "Now you're immortal, son."

Talking about Ron Yeats, it was because of an interview I did with Ron that Bill and I fell out for one of the few times this happened. I had known Ron since his Dundee United days and always had a chat when I saw him before or after games or training. On this occasion I did a short item on him in *The Weekly News*. I still don't know what his manager read into it, but a few days after it appeared I was walking along a corridor at Anfield when a raging Shankly came up to me shouting about 'bloody Press men' talking to his player without permission.

I had often talked to Liverpool players without permission because I knew they were wise about interviews. I don't know how far their manager would have gone, but he was in a real rage and maybe it was fortunate for both of us that director T V Williams, stepped between us and cooled things down.

Bill's home overlooked Everton's training ground at Bellfield and it was said he would look into the ground when the bitter local rivals were training. I rate this an apocryphal story because, having been in his house, I reckon he'd have had to be about 12 feet tall or to have climbed on to the top of a wardrobe to have a look! But it did the Shankly folklore no harm. Actually my visits to his home were to chat with his wife for a story about the non-football Bill. Ness was a wonderfully easy person to interview, with a wicked sense of humour and plenty of tales to tell.

The two best were about the Shankly courtship. This confident man who seemed to be at home in any company had wanted to chat with her when they were both in the RAF, but he had walked past her place of work daily for weeks before even speaking to her. It took even longer for him to propose a date and longer again to propose marriage.

The other myth she disposed of was that Bill had never drunk alcoholic beverages. It appeared that a doctor friend had told him that a small glass of whisky at night before bedtime was good for you, so he did this regularly, but it was a very small glass!

Yes, the man was and is a football legend – and rightly so. The only sorrow I have for him was that he left Liverpool in mixed circumstances, instead of a fanfare and recognition everywhere of his talents. To be fair, Bill suddenly decided to retire, then before he had changed his mind, had been replaced by the manager-in-waiting Bob Paisley. (unlike Alex Ferguson at Manchester United some 30 years later).

You can't really blame the club as they had to find a replacement and the boot-room Bill had created with a view to succession had Bob as No. 1 successor, Joe Fagan as No. 2, Ronnie Morgan as No. 3, Roy Evans as No. 4 (early choice Reuben Bennett, sadly had to retire because of ill-health).

Regretting his retiral decision, Bill tried to keep in touch with Liverpool, turning up for training sessions at the Melwood training ground he had been the inspiration behind creating, but that couldn't go on as the players were left confused over having to call two men 'Boss.' He did what might be called consultancy work with other clubs but I could see his heart wasn't in it. It was anchored in one place and one place only.

The boy who had started, as had his brother Bob, with a small Ayrshire club in Scotland called Glenbuck Cherrypickers (now there's a name to conjure with) was suddenly set aside. Behind him he left memories of a giant who took a going-nowhere club to the very heights and who will never be forgotten as long as the name Liverpool Football Club features in the game's history.

When he died in 1981 there was an outpouring of grief throughout the game, seldom witnessed before or since.

But before we leave Liverpool's Edinburgh trip and the tension between Shankly and Paisley there was one more shock in store. The game against Hibs successfully negotiated, we bussed back to Edinburgh Airport. I had flown reasonably regularly since my Fleet Air Arm days and as our chartered plane got into position for take-off at the end of the runway I wasn't too happy. It was a bitterly cold night with the temperature below freezing and I saw ice forming a thin film on the starboard wing – the one I could see from my seat. This was not good, but you have to trust your pilot and the controllers on the ground, which I did when it might have been better to do a bit of complaining to the crew.

So off we went down the runway – and the ice became thicker, with slivers occasionally peeling off and disappearing in the slipstream. Suddenly, the plane reared up as the brakes went on hard. There was the odd shout, and then everyone fell silent. After a brief stop, the plane was turned round and we were back at the start of the runway. I found it hard to believe the pilot was having another go, but he was.

As the engines roared up to full power we went off like we had been thrown out of a catapult. But again, as we neared the end of the runway the brakes went on hard. This time the shouts and, it has to be admitted, screams, were drowned out by the Shankly voice at its loudest.

"To hell with this! Stop. Don't even think about trying again. We don't want another Munich here. We're staying the night and you had better get us back to the main building."

I don't know whether the pilot replied or not, but the plane wheeled round and minutes later we were walking from it with a huge sense of relief and returning to our hotel – the Caledonian in the heart of Edinburgh.

Sequel? I ordered a bottle of whisky so that the Press corps could wind down before heading for bed. Suprisingly, the night porter said he didn't have any of Scotland's National Drink – and this in the centre of Scotland's capital. I had a 'discussion' with him, emphasising the shame he was bringing on our country in front of a bunch of English journalists who would delight in taking the mickey.

"Just a minute," he said, and very soon not one, but three bottles of whisky and a supply of glasses were placed on the table in front of us.

Reputation saved! Scotland's I mean!

Chapter Ten

Clough and Revie Take a Chance

As charismatic in his own way as Bill Shankly was a much younger English version – Brian Clough.

As a player he was a magnificent goal scorer for both Middlesbrough and Sunderland. Even in an era which produced many strikers of note it is amazing that he earned only two caps for his country. Too arrogant for the sensitivity of those then at the top of the game in his home country? Certainly he got up their noses as a manager, which is why he also didn't manage his country when he most certainly had the ability.

"Doesn't know half what he thinks he knows," said one pompous Football Association member to me about Clough the player and he repeated something similar when Clough the manager was proving a breath of fresh air in the game with his successful Derby County and Nottingham Forest teams. He was wanted by the public as England manager.

It was typical of an attitude which pervaded the football scene north and south of the Border, and still does in some boardrooms. No matter how successful a player / manager / coach is, he doesn't know as much about the game as directors and their like at club and national level.

Of course managers have to be reined in occasionally when, for instance, they want to spend vast sums of money a club doesn't have or demand, at national level, impossible terms – but they DO know more about the game and it is not unusual for the best of them to be arrogant and/or abrasive at times.

Clough was both of those things, but he was unquestionably outstanding as a player and as a manager. When he moved into managerial circles it was with his great friend (at the time) and calming influence Peter Taylor, at Hartlepool United. Completely overshadowed by near neighbours Sunderland and Newcastle United, Hartlepool were always struggling. I'd visited their Victoria Ground several times when working in the north-east, but this was my first visit since moving to Manchester. And what did I find? An early indication of Clough's ambition.

The manager's office had been a dingy little room in a dingy grandstand. Now it was neat and tidy, bigger and there was fresh paint brightening up the whole place. When I commented on it the Clough reply was, "You have to start somewhere and though the team's still rubbish, at least we've improved off the field."

Clough did little other than improve the standing of the club in his two years there – no sensational successes, no great headlines – but he and Peter, like Alex Ferguson, who began at Scotland's equivalent (East Stirling) at the time Clough took over Hartlepool, learned the rudiments of managing and moulded their own path to future success from small beginnings.

Though we kept in touch while Brian cut his teeth in management in the north-east, I was in Manchester and because of the solid core of teams in and around there and the Midlands (it was once estimated that 52 of the 92 league clubs of the day were in our circulation area) I didn't have time for visits. So by the next time we sat down together for a chat he was in much plusher surroundings – as manager of Derby County.

County were not where they had once been as one of the most respected club sides of them all, highlighted when they won the FA Cup in the season immediately after the Second World War. Many great players had worn the white shirt-black collar strip, not least – in fact probably most famous – Carter, Stamps and Docherty.

I had seen this magical trio play while I was in the Fleet Air Arm, training at Hednesford, not too far away for a football daft youngster to travel. Horatio (Raich) Carter, silver-haired from his young days was the wonderfully creative inside-right while Peter Doherty, the red-haired Irishman, equally skilled, could move seemingly effortlessly from penalty box to penalty box throughout the 90 minutes, was the perfect partner. And between them the goal machine that was Stamps, never honoured by his country at full international level because Doherty, being Northern Irish, couldn't play alongside him in England's national team. What he would have been like between Carter and another in support, was a situation the Selectors of the day (there was no manager then) were typically afraid to risk.

About the same time there was a parallel in Scotland. Henry Morris was a goal machine like Stamps and operated between the awesome shooting power of Charlie (Legs) Fleming and the artistry and power of Allan Brown, later a key player with Blackpool when Stanley Matthews was at his peak. Morris was awarded only one Scottish League cap, against Northern Ireland. He scored five goals in that game, but, the Selectors, like those in England (again there was no manager) didn't use him in the full Scotland team.

Why? A slightly different reason for that which kept back Stamps. Morris didn't play for Rangers, Celtic, Hearts or Hibs. Maybe in those colours he would have been chosen, but East Fife, even though they had won the Scottish Cup before the Second World War and regularly produced top class players, weren't fashionable. That was the game and its politics in my early football reporting days.

But back to Brian Clough and Derby County It was at Derby that the eccentricities of Clough's managerial approach became really apparent. Some days he would be deeply involved in training, others he wouldn't appear at the club at all. It hit home to me when I arranged a meeting with him, to which he agreed and he wasn't there when I arrived. A chat with a player brought out the information that he hadn't been seen since the end of the last game, three days earlier. Peter Taylor and others had been supervising the training and coaching.

Feeling a bit let down, I was about the head off when the man himself came bouncing into the corridor outside his office to say, "Hello young man, sorry I'm a bit late."

No information on where he had been, just a matter-of-fact throwaway line. As has probably become obvious throughout the football side of my story, actual games, though I enjoyed most of them, weren't the central feature of my work. This was interviews and stories on the people in the game; managers, players, coaches, directors in fact everyone in any way involved. Most of the stories came from observations made during games, but the football was entertainment and a means to an end.

On this particular occasion our talk turned to left winger Alan Hinton, who had been signed from Wolverhampton Wanderers. At Wolves he had been capped by England, but even though he had splashed out money on him, Clough wasn't satisfied with his performances. Hinton was powerfully built but didn't use that power and seemed at times to fade out of a game. He had pace, an eye for goal and was a good provider to others from his wide left position but lacked that fire-in-the-belly approach which Clough wanted.

"Good story," I thought and suggested to his manager that if I could say that in print it might help. I wasn't daft, nor was Clough. He had raised the subject to get his views over, I was happy to write about it. So the story duly appeared.

And Hinton? Only he knows what went on between him and his manager after publication, but suddenly he found the previously unused strength, took heavy tackles in his stride and apart from becoming a fans' favourite, won a couple more caps. It also led to a follow-up line from Clough about how happy he was that Hinton "is now showing the form I wanted from him."

Like so many managers before and since, Clough did not appreciate interference from directors and though they weren't close I was involved on occasions when both he and Don Revie proved this. In both cases I was sitting in their offices having a chat when there was a knock on the door and, without waiting, a director strode in.

The Revie incident came first. As I said "I'll pop out and come back later" the Revie response was, "You sit right where you are." Then, looking at the director who had started to say something, he raised his voice and said, "What do you think you're doing? I have an appointment with this journalist and you come barging in without being asked. Get out and stay out until I say I can see you."

To this day I can see the face of the director. It went from normal to red then pure white and without another word he left, trying and failing to slam the door behind him. After a brief silence I said to Revie, "Ah well, that's blown it . . . sorry." The reply had me chuckling for a long time afterwards.

"Don't worry, I've only just signed a new contract and sacking me for that outburst would cost them far too much. So they'll mutter away about it for a while but do nothing. It'll also show them I'm not here to be messed about."

It was also essential that Leeds kept winning – which they did. Not long after, it was déjà vu.

Sitting chatting in the manager's office at Derby County, Clough and I were interrupted by a knock on the door and a director barging in. This time I said nothing but Clough was even faster on the draw than Revie had been. Had the director not heard about waiting to be invited into the office of the manager? Who the hell did he think he was? This was a journalist and the club could do with all the publicity it could get. The director about turned and stomped his way out, red then white-faced again. I had told Clough about the Revie incident. Had he based his approach on that? Knowing him as I did, I would say it was all his own work.

There was a difference, though, "I'm in talks about a pay rise," said the manager.

"That'll test the water."

As he had already proved he was England's up-and-coming managerial star, Clough knew he had nothing to fear about repercussions – and there were none, except for similar muttering to that at Leeds. Oh . . . and he got his pay rise.

* * *

A common denominator between Clough and me was one of the great players of post-war years, Dave Mackay. I had first known the mix of power and skill when he played for the great Hearts team of Brown or Marshall; Kirk, McKenzie; Mackay, Milne, Cumming, Rutherford, Murray, Young, Wardhaugh and Hamilton. Others, like inside forwards Ian Crawford and full backs George Thomson and John Holt moved in and became regulars, but that was the top team in my memory.

They were like a breath of fresh air to the game in Scotland. Others played a fairly basic 4-2-4 system, which would probably now be described as 3-1-3-3 formation by people trying to prove how deep their knowledge of the game. In that a defensive wing-half (midfield player) would operate slightly right or left ahead of the centre-half, dropping deeper to give him cover during opposition attacks; and that one of the inside forwards would drop slightly deeper than the wingers or centre-forward to help create openings for the attackers - yes, three, or even four at times.

Puzzled? Most teams hoped the opposition was not, seemingly, realising that because they played the same way there was no great surprise involved. If there was, it was because of individual brilliance. Then along came Hearts, managed by the legendary Tommy Walker, coached by John Harvey.

Speak to people about Hearts and, if they are old enough, or have been brain-washed by fathers or grandfather, they will go on and on about the great Hearts forward trio of Alfie Conn, Willie Bauld and Jimmy Wardhaugh. While I too was a great admirer of those three, my vote as an outstanding Hearts TEAM goes to the one I have quoted. I hold the view that their playing method was down to another coach ahead of his time in John Harvey. Mind you, when I did a life story-type serialisation of the Harvey career, I fell foul of Mr Walker. Tommy, a gentleman player and hailed all round as a thoroughly decent man, objected to my interviewing John.

"I'm the manager," he said, which was a fact. "Why concentrate on the trainer?" (Which all coaches were called in those days).

"Because your career has been well publicised and it's time the Harvey career got the same treatment," I argued.

We agreed to differ and I dropped to the bottom of the Walker respect list! So much so, that I interviewed John away from Tynecastle to avoid any embarrassment to him. So I did the Harvey story, which proved popular as Hearts were riding high and he had been a top class wing-half in his playing days, winning a Scottish Cup medal with unfashionable East Fife in 1938 when they beat Kilmarnock 4-2 after a 1-1 draw in the first game.

But back to Dave Mackay. If Alex Young, a centre-forward of wonderful skill to go with his not-too-imposing physique, was the fulcrum of the wonderfully fluid attacking style of the team, the driving, hard-tackling Mackay was their inspiration. Today you read about penalty-box to penalty-box players. Dave was a bye-line to bye-line and touchline to touchline man, yet never seemed to be out of position. With John Cumming (he is still a Hearts record holder with two league titles, one Scottish Cup and four League Cups to his credit) matching his effort and power-play at the left half, it is little wonder Hearts won honour after honour in this period.

The Mackay story couldn't go on at Tynecastle. Almost from his first game, English clubs were watching him and weighing up transfer possibilities. Two things other than his ability proved his dedication to the game.

Throw-ins were just that up to then. A player took them and tried to find a colleague. Quietly, Mackay practiced a long throw. This is a common thing today, but he was the first to use it as a tactical weapon in Scotland and maybe Britain. As he matured physically, the throws got longer and when he finally produced them in competitive games it took opposition teams completely by surprise. With the old, heavy leather ball he could reach the area of the near post in the penalty area. A flick on by Wardhaugh, Young or others led to many goals.

And his application to the game didn't end there. Shin pads of the time were heavy and clumsy, yet very necessary because of the tackling with rock-solid leather boots. They had a habit too, of slipping down the inside of the woollen stockings and lodging in the top of the boot, uncomfortable and restricting when kicking a ball. Dave did something so simple it strains belief to think no one had thought of it before.

He wrapped a circle of sticky tape about an inch above the top of his boots, which stopped the shin pads slipping down too far, and had no bother after that. It also wasn't long before just about every player in the country was doing the same and sports companies began to realise they would have to update their thinking. Today's players have stockings with built-in shin pads and so on, but Dave was the first in my experience to solve a long-standing problem by the application of common-sense and a desire to improve everything about his game.

As a final compliment to that wonderful Hearts era, let me give you a statistic. In season 1957-58 they played 34 games and in the process won the title by scoring 132 goals and conceding only 29. Close to a 4-1 victory per game. Their points tally was 62 out of a possible 68; all this at a time when it was a much more level playing field financially than later when the Celtic and Rangers of that ilk could buy in players from all over the world or the best from other Scottish clubs. Both wanted Mackay and Young, both were outbid by Tottenham Hotspur and Everton respectively.

And their exploits there were of the stuff of dreams.

Dave became a key figure, if not THE key figure in a great Spurs team. Their greatest ever manager, Bill Nicholson, would never admit to having favourites. Bill was the strong, silent type who didn't gloat in success or worry about the odd upset, but he was always more talkative to me about Dave than any of his other players when we met . He had two other brilliant Scots in the Cup-winning teams of 1961 and 1962; goalkeeper Bill Brown (signed from Dundee and christened 'The Cat' because of his amazing reflexes) and John White (nicknamed 'The Ghost' because opponents found him almost impossible to mark), but Dave was, I believe, Number One.

In the early 60's the team lined up Brown, Baker, Henry, Blanchflower, Norman, Mackay; (these six the same in both finals and for a long time in the league) the flying Welshman Cliff Jones on one wing, or the other and a mix of White, Smith, Allen, Greaves, Dyson and Medwin. Jimmy Greaves was sensational as a scorer with 220 goals in his nine-years career after signing from Chelsea.

John White had been watched by Glasgow Rangers around 20 times when he played for Alloa Athletic, but they considered him too lightly built to step up to the top Scottish League. How wrong they were. John was a superb creator in the Spurs team and against any of the very physical markers he faced in the even tougher English First Division. His star was still in the ascendant when he was tragically killed when struck by lightening on a golf course when at the peak as a player.

I recall discussing a save with Bill Brown when he was with Dundee. The ball was going just wide of the post as seen from my vantage point in the Press box at Dens Park, yet Bill leapt to his left and, several feet off the ground, held the ball with both hands to a huge roar of praise from stand and terracing.

Chatting after the game I raised the point about the ball going wide.

"It was," said a smiling Bill, "but sometimes you need to show the crowd some class and that was the perfect chance. It isn't all about vital saves y'know."

I have seen some of the world's greatest goalkeepers in action since that day and, remembering Bill's words, have noted similar 'saves' from all of them. And as a final chapter to the Dave Mackay story . . .

It was freely said about his ability that he was almost finished and critics pointed to his poor display in the 1963 Scotland 9-3 defeat by England. Manager Ian McColl played two attacking wing halves in Mackay and Bert McCann and saw them and the Scots' defence completely over-run by a Bryan Douglas (Blackburn Rovers) and Greaves inspired opposition. So when Brian Clough signed Mackay from Spurs many 'experts' were smirking behind their hands at the thought that the Clough bubble had finally burst.

How wrong can you be? While admiring the Mackay all-round ability, Clough told me later, "What I realised early was that he was a brilliant reader of the game." So he moved Dave back a stage, into a sort of double centre-half role where he didn't need to work non-stop, but could assess what was going on and keep others in the picture. It was an inspired move and Derby won both the First Division title and the Texaco Cup with Mackay the driving force on the park. When Clough moved to Nottingham Forest and even greater glory, Mackay became his successor – and won the top title again for the club.

Which brings us to the other Hearts legend, The Golden Vision – Alex Young. I was there at Clyde's Shawfield Stadium in Glasgow the day he signed for Everton. It wasn't the best game on the fixture list but, advised in a telephone call by Everton manager Harry Catterick, who frequently phoned me to update the form of players in Scotland, that it might be a good one to visit, I bussed my way over.

Also there was a football writer from the *Daily Record,* Jim Rodger, nicknamed for obvious reasons, The Jolly and so well known over the years that the Press Centre at the new Hampden Park is named after him. Competitors yes, but friends too.

Catterick was there as promised and when he saw me stopping to talk with the Everton boss, Jim veered left and joined us. It was over an hour after the end of the game and while I didn't have a report to write, Jim had finished being in touch with the Record's sister paper, *The Sunday Mail.* We were the only two football writers left.

"Seeing you're both here I'll tell you both," said Catterick, "I have signed Alex Young." We duly noted this, asked a few questions "the fee?" – which we were told was £40,000.

Jim immediately bustled off to phone the Sunday Mail. I paused to ask Harry, whom I knew well from his phone calls and previous visits to Scotland, how things were at Goodison Park.

"Pretty fair . . . we're doing a bit of team building," he answered.

"In Scotland again?" I queried.

"Well now," he answered.

"Which means?"

"That I've done a double deal with Hearts today. As well as Alex Young I've signed the left back, George Thompson."

"And both for £40,000?"

"Well the total for the two is actually £55,000."

So next day the *Sunday Post* had the exclusive news of a DOUBLE signing as opposed to others reporting the Alex Young move.

I was lucky? Well, maybe. The right place right time plus a bit of luck never hurt anyone.

As everyone of Everton persuasion knows, Alex went on to become such a legend at Goodison Park that a television play; *The Golden Vision* (which Spurs captain Danny Blanchflower had christened him) was based on his career there.

Not that he started well. Fair-haired, looking about 12 years old facially and with a physique at odds with the average heftily-built, powerful centre-forwards of the day – and only 5ft 8ins tall. Though magnificent in the air, the Goodison fans openly questioned Catterick's sanity in making this signing and Young's quality as he struggled to fit in. Who could blame them when this Scotsman was taking up a position previously occupied by real legends in the game, Dixie Dean and Tommy Lawton?

What they hadn't reckoned with was Young's determination to succeed. His footballing gifts were suddenly to blossom when he found form in a team which included people like Ray Wilson, Brian Labone, Colin Harvey, Tommy Wright, fellow-Scots Jimmy Gabriel and Alex Scott and Derek Temple. This team, with additions and subtractions, won the FA Cup in 1966 and the league title in '63 and '70.

Having been friendly with Alex in Scotland, we often met when I worked out of Manchester. There was a spell when critics were saying he didn't like it when the opposition went physical on him. That was rubbish. He wasn't stupid, but I recall discussing the issue with him at the Belfield training ground, knowing that he had the misfortune to have feet which blistered so easily that his boots were often full of blood at the end of a game. He rolled up his track suit trouser and showed me his legs. There wasn't a square inch of them clear of bruises or cuts caused by heavy tackles.

Colour photography wasn't 'in' with newspapers then, but if it had been Alex's 'patter' of blue, green, Red and purple legs would have made a striking feature!

Typically, his comment was "Looks like I dodge tackles, doesn't it."

Goodison Park was surrounded by Coronation Street types of roads and I used to park wherever I could get a space. On this particular occasion, after a night game and chats with players and officials, I was leaving for home at around 11 o'clock. Footsteps behind me, made me wary, it wasn't a bad area, but it was not all that well lit. It probably wasn't wise, but I stopped, turned and went face to face with my follower, a well-built man wearing an Everton scarf.

"Got a problem?" I asked.

"No," he answered, "I just want to shake your hand."

Completely mystified, I asked "Why?"

"Because I saw you shaking hands with Alex Young and I want to shake the hand of someone who knows him that well," was the stunning (to me) reply.

Now shaking hands with a bloke who has been following you along a darkened street might not be considered advisable, but I was so surprised I did it anyway. Result? He politely said, "Thanks, I'll never forget that," and disappeared into the night. It must come close to being the greatest example of hero-worship I ever came across.

. . . or maybe not . . . It was after a visit to Anfield on an ordinary mid-week day and as I went to get my car Bill Shankly and I stopped for a brief chat. That over I continued on my way. My car was parked in a side street as I'd stopped at a corner shop to buy a newspaper on my way to Anfield. I'd gone a very short distance before I realised a car was crawling along on the road just behind me. Not just any old car, but a gleaming silver Mercedes. Now, this was Liverpool, a big city and in big cities you were extra careful of unusual happenings, which this was.

As I was wondering whether to take to my heels or stop and ask what was going on, the car accelerated and stopped, engine still purring. As I drew level the front window was wound down and in a totally Merseyside accent I was asked, by someone if I "had a minute."

Still suspicious and not a little worried, I asked "why?

The rear window wound down a little and a different voice said "Saw you speaking to Mr Shankly. You a pal of his being a Jock?"

Still nervy, I said "not really" and explained we were acquaintances because of my job as a football writer.

Then came the surprise, "He's the greatest . . . Just wanted to speak to somebody who knew him well," said the back seat voice. "You get on with him?"

I was able to say yes, told a couple of legendary stories about Bill and threw one in about his brother Bob.

"OK," said the voice, the window was shut and the car accelerated away. I later found out that the car belonged to a gentleman (?) well known to the police, high in the criminal fraternity on Merseyside and an acknowledged Liverpool fan. Probably because of his 'business' he either didn't go to the Liverpool games or did so, low profile, and hadn't met the legend who was also his hero.

But how did he know I was a Scot? All I had said before he tagged me was "Why?" Had he checked me out? Was it just an accident that he happened to be where he was on the particular day? I don't know because I felt it best not to pursue the matter. But he must also be high on the list of the great fans I have known.

Chapter Eleven

Catterick and Shankly

What must be remembered in all of this is that, when I started out in my life as a reporter, football was popular with huge crowds at the 'big' games (138,000 at Scotland's Hampden Park was regular when such as England were in opposition).

There were no floodlights (a puzzled club director once said to me, "How can you possibly have enough light from electric bulbs to make it bright enough to play football in?"); more terracing with rib-bending crush barriers than stands or enclosures so that most people were soaked if it rained. The ball was made of leather and had a laced-up opening hiding an attached tube for blowing it up to the required pressure. If that lace caught you on the forehead when heading the ball (which became heavier as it absorbed water on rainy days) you were lucky to be only stunned.

My playing career peaked at junior football level but I was once rushed to Dr Gray's Hospital in Elgin after heading a ball wrongly and suffering concussion which left me with a headache that lasted for several days.

Players' equipment?

Think woollen jerseys and cotton shorts, woollen stockings and heavy leather boots with toe-caps so solid that if an opposition player landed on them no damage was done to your foot. If you caught an opponent with them in a tackle severe bruising was the least he could hope for.

Oh yes, there were shin-pads. Canes inserted in a leather cover were popular with top players, but lesser mortals often got by with copies of boys' magazines such as *The Wizard*, *The Hotspur* and/or *The Rover* stuffed down the front of the stocking. It is an undeniable fact that today's players, with their light-weight strips, shorts and stockings, not to mention boots that are more like slippers, cut dangerously low and made of materials which are stronger than steel as are shin-pads, don't even begin to know what it was like from the time football began to the 1940s and 1950s.

Bill Shankly was one who did know the difference. He had played in the old-fashioned gear and saw the gradual development of the new equipment as he managed Liverpool.

"Because as a kid I had to blow up footballs, I only needed to hold a ball and squeeze it to know whether it was too hard, or soft," he once told me.

He proved he was right when Liverpool made an early European excursion to Switzerland. I came across him in the tunnel leading to the pitch before the game. The teams were lined up to make their entrance into the arena, but he was bouncing the match ball up and down which he had somehow purloined from the referee,

"It's too soft," he said to the assembled officials and representatives of both clubs.

The referee tried to get the ball back, but he blocked him and kept bouncing it and saying again and again "It's too soft."

Finally he gave it up to the referee and they both disappeared into the groundsman's quarters. Five minutes later, with everyone champing at the bit, they emerged with Shankly triumphantly announcing "I told you . . . it was too soft. The ref proved it." He later told me that even if he always bounced the ball before a game, more often than not it was at the perfect pressure.

"But even then it puts a wee bit of doubt in their (the opposition) minds and that's a plus for us," he said. More Shankly psychology!

As was illustrated again when Liverpool entered late autumn in the unaccustomed position of being in the bottom half of the league table, while Sheffield United were top and going well. Just before the two clubs met at Anfield, I asked him what had gone wrong with his team, which normally was in the top four all season. In his philosopher mood, he said solemnly, "There's wheat and there's chaff, sir. And when the wind gets strong and the going gets tough, the chaff blows away but the wheat survives and gets stronger."

Sheffield United were relegated that season, Liverpool won the title.

Earlier I mentioned Harry Catterick, manager of Everton. Every time I went to Anfield and met Bill Shankly his first question was, "Been over the road then?" meaning, of course, Everton's magnificent Bellfield training ground. And the follow up question, as he leaned closer to check, was always the same, "Had a drink maybe?"

The reason for that is that once, yes once, a former Weekly News man had arrived for a chat with Bill after having been at Goodison, Everton's home ground, where he was given a small glass of sherry. As he wasn't driving, but had travelled from Manchester by train, it didn't matter, but to Bill it proved a bias towards his greatest rivals as he would never even think of providing an alcoholic beverage to Press men. As I always travelled by car to Liverpool I never had a drink, so was always able to answer "no." The question though was, inevitably, asked.

But, back to Harry Catterick. His ability as a player is always vastly under-estimated because that career mostly blossomed during the Second World War when far more important issues than football captured the headlines. During the war years he scored 59 goals in nearly 80 games for Everton; an exceptional haul for any centre-forward, especially with a club that had such true greats as Dixie Dean and Tommy Lawton in their ranks at different times.

When Catterick finally got his post-war chance with the Goodison club he was 27 years old and averaged a creditable goal every three games. That said, it is a fact that his talent on the field was far outweighed by his knowledge of the game and his ability to build a successful team.

His father coached Stockport County where Harry started his career as an amateur and after playing for Everton he moved to Crewe Alexandra, where he was manager after finishing his playing career. After a managerial apprenticeship with Crewe, Stockport and Sheffield Wednesday, Everton beckoned him back into the fold with the instruction to produce a football team which had not only to be successful, but also to play football which was attractive and a pleasure to watch.

Did he succeed? Yes, in every way. Twice he took the First Division championship to Goodison Park, in season 1962-63 and 1969-70;

once the FA Cup in 1966, when they beat Sheffield Wednesday 3-2 with two Trebilcock and one Temple goals and once the Charity Shield. In addition, Everton were FA Cup runners-up in 1968, when they lost 1-0 to West Bromwich Albion, with almost inevitably a Geoff Astle goal the clincher. Twice there were European Cup nights, once a Cup Winners Cup adventure and three times involvement in the Fairs Cup.

A record I am sure almost any club manager would be proud of, which Harry undoubtedly was. But always there seemed to be that element of the Everton support ready to criticise him. He had a low profile type of approach to life, he didn't make friends easily and he could undoubtedly be moody.

However, the criticism seemed always to be there and the man himself both knew it and resented it. That was made clear immediately after the final whistle in the 1966 Cup final. The Cup was being passed around the successful Everton players and finally got to the manager. As I watched I was sure he didn't so much display it to the Blues support as thrust it at them in the equivalent of a two-fingered gesture. In the dressing room afterwards; those were the days when football was still a game and reporters could get into the winning and losing dressing room, I waited until he was on his own and put the question to him: did he thrust the Cup at the Everton fans, not just display it?

"You noticed did you?" he said. "Yes, I definitely did.

"Why?"

"Because these are the same lot who were screaming abuse at me earlier in the season. Who the hell do they think they are?"

Actually, that was pretty typical of the Catterick approach to life. Even with his players he didn't get really close. He admitted to me that he had some favourites, "but they'll never know who they are."

I was fortunate that our acquaintanceship went back some years and that I had helped him with information on players when he was scouting in Scotland. Why? Because he had a deep dislike and distrust of 'The Press' and an even greater dislike of television. He asked me once what I thought of the then new trend of televising games. Knowing the man I didn't answer directly but replied with my own question – "Why?"

"Because if that ever becomes a regular thing every team manager will know everything about the opposition team's style and players. It'll ruin the game," he said.

He was a master at manipulating Press stories so they were what he wanted to see, not what certain reporters tried to make of them. Strangely I didn't object to this because I wasn't in the hard news side of the business, but relied mostly on personal tales and background stories. The fact that he gave out team lists in alphabetical order rather than in the traditional goalkeeper; full backs; half backs and forwards formation, didn't affect me.

He produced many good tales for my publication because of his attitude. There was the one about Joe Royle, the big centre-forward who went on to become an Everton legend.

It started with his comment, "Big Joe doesn't use his size enough."

"Which means?" I queried.

"That if he ever gets really angry and starts getting stuck in, he'll knock defenders about instead of letting them boss him."

I did the story on the lines of "If Joe Royle every gets angry . . ." And Joe reacted by using his physical attributes more and becoming a better player – not always but often enough to become an England international.

Alex Young came in for a bit of the psychology too.

"A great player . . . at Goodison," was the Catterick opening.

"Which means you have doubts about his away form?" I countered.

"I reckon so." Came the answer. "He'll have to get into the game more when we are away because it isn't happening just now."

Actually, there had been only a slight dip in Young's scoring rate away, but the Catterick approach was to 'retaliate first' as the saying goes, and make sure Alex got back on the goal standard quickly. He did!

While other coaches and managers would be out on the training pitch working with everyone from the young apprentices to seasoned internationals, the Catterick approach was to watch from his seat in the corner of his office at Bellfield as everyone went through their paces. It was left to the coaching staff he appointed, Tommy Egglestone, Wilf Dixon and so on, to do the training, but because he missed nothing from his eyrie one storey up at Bellfield, and he talked regularly to the coaches, he knew all he needed to about every player.

Not that he was always serious. On a trip to Iceland for a European tie we sat together watching a party in full swing at a local hostelry. He sang along with the choruses we knew, even though neither of us had taken an alcoholic drink. The reason was simple. In Reykavik, even all over Iceland at the time to my knowledge, you weren't allowed to drink alcoholic beverages, other than the weakest beer that was ever to pass my lips.

And suddenly the typical Catterick approach kicked in.

"Noticed anything?" he said.

"Such as?" I answered.

"That most locals are getting steadily more and more drunk."

I looked around and it was true. "On that beer," I said, "it's impossible."

"So you haven't noticed anything else," he said.

Again "Such as?"

"The size of the handbags the women are carrying."

Actually I had, but thought it was something of a local fashion statement.

"And out of those bags at regular intervals came bottles, after which they pour something into the beer, after which everyone gets steadily 'merrier'," he said.

So, in investigative mode he asked the next man who asked for his autograph what was going on. In perfect English the reply was that if there was a couple or a group, the women carried in their huge handbags, bottles of spirits, whisky (the favourite), vodka, rum or whatever to 'top up' the weak beer and produce a blend that guaranteed relaxation!

"Could I arrange for you to have a supply?" asked our informant.

We agreed it would be churlish to refuse – and almost immediately, the party at the next table started topping up our beer. We then joined more intensely in the sing-song and the general chat and were rather later to bed than we had assumed at the start of the evening.

This was the period in England when there was probably the greatest number of outstanding British-born managers in charge ever and Harry Catterick was undoubtedly one of them. He died of a heart attack aged 65 while watching a game at Goodison Park in 1985. The fans he thought didn't like him were not slow to praise his outstanding contribution to the history of the club. Would he have liked that? Being the man he was and a real friend of mine he would privately have loved the praise, but publicly admitted nothing.

'You never lose it' – the manager who created a great Liverpool FC, Bill Shankly, leaves a young player sprawling in a training ground game.

Everton and Liverpool captains, Alan Ball (left) and Ron Yeats, lead out their teams for a Merseyside derby.

Right :
George Anderson, the
bowler-hatted boss of
Dundee who performed
the football miracle of
signing Billy Steel.

Below : Billy Steel.

Dave Mackay, another of the game's legendary
figures with Hearts, Spurs and Derby County.
Note the heavy leather ball he is carrying.

A young Bobby Collins trots out for Celtic. It was
the start of a glittering career, particularly with
Leeds United as Don Revie acknowledged.

Above :
Jock Stein became a true
great by leading Celtic
to European Cup glory.

Right :
It was said Jim
McLean, who made
Dundee United a
power in the land,
was dour – but this
proves he could
have a laugh!

Welcoming Billy Steel (second left) to Dundee when on holiday
from his new home in America – (left) Tommy Gemmell,
player and manager at Dens Park, but earlier a European Cup
winner with Celtic; Tommy Gallacher, (standing) a team-
mate of Steel's and later sports columnist with *The Courier*,
Dundee; Willie Wallace, a coach at Dundee and a team-
mate of Gemmell's when Celtic won the European Cup and
Hugh Robertson, coach at Dundee who, as a player, was
outside-left when Dundee won the First Division title.

Mildred meets me on my return from
the 1982 World Cup in Spain.

A good evening was had by all – George Best,
the author, Alex Harly (then Manchester City),
Harry Gregg (Manchester United).

Bob Shankly, manager of Dundee when they
won the championship for the only time. As
good as, or better than, brother Bill?

Pat Crerand (seated) of Celtic, Manchester United
and Scotland made the ball do the work. Here, he
and Ian have a chat about football – what else?

Ian and a Press colleague are on their way into East Germany
via Checkpoint Charlie – and problems lie ahead.

Ally McLeod and his Tartan Army scarf. A top
Scotland manager let down by his players.

Chapter Twelve

Superstitious Don Revie

Around thirty miles west I was in Liverpool, a bit further east and it was Leeds. Both these cities had teams vying for top honours in English and increasingly, European football.

While Liverpool were in the exciting eras of Catterick and Shankly – that's in strictly alphabetical order in case I am accused of bias! – Leeds United's renaissance was in the hands of Don Revie.

Don had been a centre-forward with a difference when he made his name for Manchester City. He lay deeper than usual not so much spearhead, as was the fashion of the time, but as a provider for players who made use of his ability to find defensive gaps in opposition defences, get on to his passes and score goals. (Hidgekuti of the wonderful Hungarian team which shattered England 6-3 at Wembley and Scotland 4-2 at Hampden, in the 1950s played a similar role)

He was capped six times for England, played in a losing Cup final for City against Newcastle in 1955 (3-1) and a winning final against Birmingham City the next year – a victorious 3-1 this time.

His wife Elsie, was Scottish and the player he often told me was 'a genius' was alongside him with City. This was Scot Bobby Johnstone, who had been signed from the famous Hibernian forward line, often rated the best front five ever in Scotland; Gordon Smith, Johnstone, Lawrie Reilly, Eddie Turnbull and Willie Ormond.

So it looked as though, with that tartan background, I would find it easy to get on with him. Not so. His first comment when we met at Elland Road, the Leeds ground was "I can't be sure I can trust you!"

I naturally asked why and was told someone had said to "watch out for him . . . " As he never told me who, I can't name names, even though I have a pretty good idea. I confronted my 'suspect' later and am satisfied I got it right.

However, Don and I went on to be good friends when I proved to him that I could be trusted. Not that he was popular with other managers. In fact, great though they all were in their job, the private back-biting that went on was consistent and remarkable.

"Did you hear that . . . ?"

"Is it right that . . . "

Rumour after rumour came my way as I 'did the rounds' of the managerial starts of their day. How true were they? Mostly, not at all. Mostly! Those that were weren't for newspaper consumption, certainly not newspapers of the time.

Probably the thing I recall most about Don is his superstitions. Almost all sportsmen have them, but few as many as him. The first time I visited Elland Road and his new office, wood panelled, carpeted and with a decent sized desk behind which he sat, he tapped the door of one cupboard and it swung open to reveal a range of bottles containing all sorts of alcoholic drink.

"What'll you have?" he asked. I replied that I never had a drink (alcoholic) when I was driving, but he insisted. Finally I agreed to have a small sherry. His idea of small and mine didn't concur, so I sat for about an hour chatting and sipping. What he didn't know was that there were two drinks that affected me more quickly than others, white wine and – you've guessed it – sherry.

By the time I had finished my drink I was in a relaxed state. That meant I wasn't going to drive for at least a couple of hours, which was the time I reckoned would see me clear of any effects of the drink. So off we went on a tour of various parts of the stadium. Among the sights, and it was a sight, was the massage room where a player was on a table completely naked having a massage from a heavily built operator who was, it seemed to me, giving him a real hammering!

"Keeps them supple," was Don's only comment.

My thought was, "If they survive."

But back to the sherry. Next day, Leeds played and won. So on my next visit it was insisted that I have a sherry and that we tour the stadium again in exactly the order we did the previous time. We duly did – and Leeds won again.

From then on, I had my small sherry every visit and insisted it had to be small – and because they were a good team Leeds kept winning.

But that was only one of Don's superstitions. I was involved in another one, this time to do with food. Due to go to a Leeds game one night, I took a call from Don at the office in Manchester asking me to join the players and staff for a light snack before the game. I duly turned up at their hotel in Leeds city centre and was given a plate of chicken and vegetables, followed in my case, by a cup of tea. Again they won and the very next night game I got a call at the office asking me to join the team for a light snack. This time I had arranged to go elsewhere so despite lengthy pleas from Don I turned down the invitation. Fortunately Leeds won again and I managed to persuade him that this particular superstition was outweighed by the fact they would win most games anyway.

Not superstitious, but a key figure in Leeds' rise to the top was a little fellow who looked as though a strong wind would blow him away. He was, like an uncle of mine who had been an Army regular in the early 1900s, as tough as anyone I have ever met. Maybe he hadn't the stature, but what there was seemed the equivalent of steel springs.

The name was Les Cocker and to underline his ability to keep players fit Alf Ramsey, a superb judge of men, chose him as his trainer with England. I was told Les had been, in the Second World War, a member of the Long Range Desert Group. This bunch of men thought nothing of travelling hundreds of North African desert miles to get behind enemy lines, blow up ammunition and supply dumps, destroy aeroplanes and any other weapons of war available and scoot back to base in their Jeeps or whatever. Was he one of them? He refused even to talk about it.

But you had to be tough to be allowed into that group – and Les was tough. I saw him take groups of super fit footballers on runs where he led all the time and dared them to fall behind; do exercises that would crucify the average fit person – and do all of them with the players. He was much older than most of them and senior to all.

He became a friend and I am proud to say that. He didn't want anything written about him and hard though I tried to persuade him, when I spotted something that would have made a good story, he always refused.

He was the one who went onto the park to check on injured players. What I noticed several times was how he was very careful to place his trainer's bag with the lettering of the manufacturers pointing straight at the television cameras. On instruction? Obviously. And paid a fee for the publicity? I never did find out, but I have a good idea. As a final piece of Revie-Cocker information I go back to a night in Belgium when Leeds were on European duty.

As we trooped off the bus taking us to Anderlecht's ground, I was chatting with a director. We were behind the players and staff. At the gate there was a hold-up. I later found out that a gent with an armband and the attitude of a dictator was refusing to accept that this was the Leeds party and was insisting that he wasn't being shown the correct identification. (which I later ascertained, he was.) He wouldn't open the door leading us into the stadium, until he suddenly fell to the ground, and Mssrs Revie and Cocker opened it for him. When the attendant got to his feet he was shouting about having been knocked over (his words were gibberish to me, but were translated by a local journalist).

"Knocked over, how?" I queried.

"Punched in the stomach by a member of the Leeds party," I was told.

Naturally the travelling Press Corps investigated, but no one with the home club, or anyone else for that matter, would back up the man's story. We also had chats with the Leeds players at or near the front of the queue and, I almost said naturally, they saw nothing.

Over to Don and Les. "He just suddenly went down," said the manager.

"He was stopping us getting into the ground, but when he fell over we opened the gate," was the trainer's version.

So it was a non-story? No violence? A fortunate (for Leeds) tumble? Allegedly. But the man did fall very suddenly, the Leeds party were getting increasingly angry at the delay and they usually tackled problems head on.

Ah well . . . The Leeds team of that time was the best in the club's history. Sprake, Reaney, Cooper, Bremner, Madeley, Charlton, Hunter, Lorimer, Giles, Jones, Clarke, Gray and others wrote their names into football history.

On the way to that polished and highly successful team, one man in particular gave them a flying start. Bobby Collins was a Scot I first came across playing junior football in Glasgow. At 5ft 4ins and up towards the 10st mark, when many were 12st and eight to ten inches taller, he had to be extra tough to cope at that level – and he was. They took no prisoners in junior west of Scotland football and any sign of weakness saw a player drop off the radar.

Bobby showed no sign of weakness and opposition players fancying their chances of 'sorting out the wee barra' were quickly put in their place because, despite his stature, Bobby, in common with Les Cocker, was like Scotland's 'other national drink' (Irn Bru) 'made of girders'!

His career is well documented; a ridiculously low 31 caps between 1951 and 1965, his debut for Celtic as an 18 year old in August 1949 and final game of 800 (200 goals) for Oldham Athletic in April 1973; playing for Everton before moving to Leeds in 1962.

Statistics though, don't look at the person, and although they give an idea of the quality of the man they are only a hint. I doubt if anywhere in the history of the game have so many who became 'greats' paid tribute to one man, Collins, for getting them there.

I met Don Revie not long after he signed Collins for Leeds and he admitted he was baffled that he had been able to sign him from Everton (then miles ahead of Leeds in the game) and "can't believe my luck in getting him." When Bobby arrived at Leeds they were as good as in the Third Division. Nine unbeaten games later they had stayed in the Second Division and, seemingly in next to no time, they were in the top league.

Many shared the honours in making them what they became, but years later, when I visited Revie in his home in Kinross where he finally succumbed to the ravages of motor neuron disease, he ended a lengthy memory recall of his great players with, "but there was one above them all. Bobby Collins. He gave us the fire we needed, the start we needed, he brought on the young lads who became household names, and he was an inspiration."

There are many tales of this little spitfire with magic in his size four boots 'sorting out' situations on the park where a team-mate was 'put upon'.

It is reckoned by some that Norman Hunter (along with Tommy Smith at Liverpool and Nobby Stiles at Manchester United) were the hardest men of their time. I don't think that is the full list, but these men were hard. Yet Hunter, in one game, felt he had been unfairly dealt with by an opponent. Like a flash Collins advised him to leave the player to him. Next thing, that player was flat out and an innocent Hunter was being lectured by the referee while perpetrator Collins, a long way away by this time, was standing smiling and chatting with a team-mate.

Throughout his career, Bobby and I were on friendly terms - except once. This came about after Johnny Giles joined Leeds from Manchester United. Several chats with Don Revie made it clear that Giles was a long term investment as Collins' successor. I decided to write a carefully worded piece about this, indicating quite clearly that I was not writing the Collins obituary as a Leeds player, merely looking well ahead.

I had seen Bobby's temper on the park and his philosophy of heading straight for what he perceived as trouble. This time, as was my habit, I was inside Elland Road a good 90 minutes before the game started, to chat with contacts. The manager stopped for a minute and it was a good job he did. Bobby came from behind me and whirled me round, I looked at the angry white face and stepped back as I anticipated a 'collision'. Like a flash Revie stepped between us, grabbing Bobby by the shoulders.

"Calm down, calm down," he kept repeating, while I was subjected to a rant on the lines of, "How the hell can you say I'm finished, who the hell do you think you are, I've got years yet, I thought you were a pal."

This got me going. I had made sure I was saying nothing of the kind and was needled at the Collins attitude. So, I pulled the manager aside and had my own rant.

"Typical . . . you didn't read the bloody thing properly . . . you're like the rest . . . blame the reporter."

I don't know what would have happened if Revie hadn't got between us again, but I had the same Scottish temper as Collins and we were both spoiling for a set to. Whatever – my words did seem to get through and the player was led away by his boss.

Believing, like Collins, that it's often best to go to a flash point, I waited for him at the end of the game, first asking his manager to make sure we could meet. We both ended in the manager's office, where he had looked out the article. Bobby had wound down after the game and this time he listened to me. I didn't expect an apology and didn't get one, but next time we met things were back to normal between us.

Oh . . . and Johnny Giles became a magnificent successor to Collins – but not for a reasonable time after the article appeared.

* * *

Strangely enough, though I wasn't a confrontational person, I did have another head-to-head disagreement before the Collins spat. Again it was with a friend, before and after, though not on the day.

While Bob Shankly was managing the long-now-defunct Third Lanark in Glasgow, his centre-half George McCallum suffered a knee ligament injury. In those days this was considered a career-ending tragedy. However, Thirds had as their physiotherapist at the time a man I consider the best I ever came in contact with. Tom McNiven, was a quiet spoken, slim, blonde-haired young man who knew seemingly everything about the human body, especially it's muscle and bone frailties.

Had he been a pushy type I'm sure his name would be known in every treatment room in the game, but he was content to do his job and let his cures speak for themselves. He actually cured the McCallum knee – so much so that the impossible happened and the centre-half played again.

Knowing I would get nothing in terms of publicity out of Tom I decided to visit McCallum at his home when I knew his comeback was imminent. He lavished praise on the physio and detailed the route his treatment had taken. When the story appeared I got a Shankly summons to his office at Thirds' Cathkin Park on the south side of Glasgow.

As soon as I walked through the door he exploded. How dare I speak to one of his players without permission? Who did I think I was writing stories like that without his permission? It went on until he ran out of words which gave me the opportunity to point out that he had never once objected to me talking to any of his players before and that his physio deserved praise he would never lavish on himself. When it was my turn to run out of words I was ordered to "get out" and did, fuming.

I was still angry when the phone rang in the Port Dundas Street office next day.

"Shankly here, if you out this way today, drop into Cathkin," was the invitation.

In a stupid sort of 'dummy out of the pram' huff, I said I couldn't visit until a few days later.

"See you then," was the answer.

A few days later I did 'drop in' and was immediately greeted with "Just wanted to say I appreciate your reason for that story. I was in a bit of a mood that day."

Oh – and this reminds me of one other link between the Shankly brothers, Cathkin and Anfield which didn't involve an argument. When Bill had left Liverpool and we were having a cup of tea in his home near Everton's training ground, the name of Joe McInnes cropped up.

Third Lanark outside left Joe was as near a genius with the ball as I have ever seen. The ground behind the Cathkin stand was rutted where rainwater had gouged groves. Sometimes the Thirds players would kick a ball about there and my abiding memory is of McInnes getting on the ball and keeping it at this feet no matter who tried to take it off him. How he avoided the ruts and the tackles baffled me – and all the other players.

On match day and if he was in the mood, he was the ultimate crowd-pleaser.

"I," said Bill "was looking for a left winger who could hold the ball, who could keep it while we sorted ourselves out in a game. Joe seemed perfect for the job."

"But he never arrived at Anfield?" I queried.

"No. We checked him out and weren't satisfied that he was committed enough, didn't measure up to all our standards, so we left it, but he was a helluva player."

Not long afterwards, Liverpool signed Peter Thompson from Preston North End, a player who could keep the ball if Liverpool were 'sorting themselves out' and who was 'committed to the cause'.

Chapter Thirteen

Hunting in Pairs

Men in charge of the playing side of football clubs tend to hunt in pairs.

There was Matt Busby and Jimmy Murphy, Jock Stein and Sean Fallon, Brian Clough and Peter Taylor and many others of my acquaintance, but by a whisker my top two were, Joe Mercer and Malcolm Allison. They took over when Manchester City were the second best team in the city and also-rans in English football in general (OK I know Manchester United are Salford-based, but I lived in Chorlton-cum-Hardy for 17 years and could reach both in about the same time without feeling I had crossed any boundaries).

Others would choose any of the other three pairs I mention (or others) but my choice is based not only on success but on the explosive quality of that success over relatively few seasons.

My connection with the Mercer-Allison pairing actually started on a station platform in London and didn't at first involve them personally. At a meeting in London I picked up a hint that Manchester City were about to appoint a new manager. My informant named Joe Mercer 'and a young number two.' As luck would have it, next day I was travelling north on the same train as Mr Albert Alexander, the then chairman of City.

A small, dapper, immaculately dressed man with a ready smile and a brisk manner, Mr Alexander was also adept at telling you only what he wanted you to know, not what you really wanted to know. So, when I approached him he was his usual polite self, but didn't stop walking on his way to his booked first class seat.

"Am I right in thinking you have or are about to appoint a new manager for the club?" I queried.

He paused in his stride for a second, then answered, "All things are possible, but I have no news for you in that direction."

"I've even heard it will be Joe Mercer."

"As I say, I have no news. See me back in Manchester and we'll discuss your questions."

With that he was into his carriage, which was full, while I made my way to mine.

In Manchester I found he had hustled off the train at Stockport with a group of friends. Within days he called a Press conference and it was duly announced that Joe Mercer had been appointed manager with Malcolm Allison as his assistant. Afterwards he singled me out to tell me he genuinely hadn't been able to answer my question because, although there was broad agreement about the appointment, it hadn't been finalised and to have said anything positive would have been very risky. I took his point.

This was 1965 and I had met Joe several years before and had visited him several times when he managed Aston Villa. In his playing career as a commanding wing-half (midfield man in today's jargon) he moved into the big-time with Everton before being transferred, for £9,000, to Arsenal, captaining them and bringing success in league and FA Cup.

Like so many of his generation he would have achieved even greater club success and certainly many, many more official appearances for England than his five pre-war caps had the war and military service not interrupted. He had 25 England honours in war-time, including captaining his country, but they are never counted in official records. For obvious reasons international games were few and far between. By today's standards and the proliferation of games between countries I believe Joe's 30 honours would have been at least trebled.

However, his success as a player was not reflected in his early days as a manager. His record with Sheffield United or Villa wasn't good. In fact, both were relegated when he was in charge. But a closer study makes it clear that he had the task of re-building at both places and that he left behind a considerable array of young talent heading for the first teams.

Behind the melon-slice smile and the seemingly light-hearted approach to life, Joe was a serious thinker on the game. I remember, for instance, one chat at Villa's training ground where a young black lad was performing amazing tricks with the ball. It was a time when the children of West Indian and African immigrants were thin on the ground at football clubs, but Villa had this lad and one or two others.

"Amazing talent" I said to Joe about the youngster.

"Yes," was the answer "but he'll never make it into the first team. He doesn't like training and he doesn't like being tackled."

"Just wait though. When his children and their children take to football, they will have learned the British way of playing because they'll be British, but they'll still have those in-built skills. It'll all come together and our teams will have plenty of black youngsters playing regularly."

How's that for a peek into the future when you consider how many black players have hit the very top in the years since? Another plus for me was that when Joe's appointment was confirmed, he moved into a house within half-a-mile of mine in Chorlton and not far from Matt Busby's home, so I had many a visit to both, well away from the hustle and bustle of training grounds and stadiums.

But Malcolm Allison as his assistant? Who? Actually, I knew of Malcolm through our London office. 'A West Ham player and promising centre-half, hit by the terrible scourge of the day, tuberculosis and lost a lung. Playing career ended but proving a promising coach, though not yet 40 and claimed by many to be the man behind the rise and rise of West Ham and England World Cup winning captain, Bobby Moore.'

Then I met him. Tall, definitely handsome – wearing a fedora hat, a coat and suit worthy of the fashion pages of any magazine and smoking a huge cigar. Not only that – he was born on exactly the same day as me, 5 September, 1927. To put it mildly he was not a typical example of managers and coaches of that time, even though we were into the Beatles-Carnaby Street era.

One (envious?) manager of a club not too far from Manchester summed up the new arrival as a "flash bastard." I had a smile over that one, especially considering few people dressed as drably as that manager did!

Mercer and Allison were a very unlikely pairing and in the end that may have been the secret of their success. They knew what they wanted by way of a team – Joe's values rooted in experience of the game, Malcolm a new thinker, seeing different formations, different use of players. Basically they had a 4-2-4 formation, but with players who could change the permutation in an instant.

Colin Bell signed from Bury when he was 20 for £45,000 and described by Allison as 'nothing special' in an attempt to put an increasing army of admirers off the scent, while Joe and he tried to persuade the Board to raise what was a huge sum of money at the time to sign him. Only thing was that, even though Malcolm had a mesmeric way of talking, his assessment of Bell was so obviously false to all who heard him, which included me several times, that very few used his quotes.

Colin was a man of few words but fantastic energy. He was, to me, in the same class as Peter Doherty, who formed that wonderful partnership with Raich Carter and Stamps at Derby some 20 years earlier – and who also, of course, played with Manchester City for a time.

In fact so intrigued was a local university with the Bell energy levels that they plugged him into a machine which tested his breathing, heart-beat and so on. The result was amazing proof that few people were such complete physical specimens, built to go on and on when their energy levels were tested while ordinary, even very fit people, would have to rest. The Maine Road supporters nicknamed him Nijinsky after a race-horse with the speed and stamina to outclass every opponent.

Bell is also rated by many as being the greatest player in City's history, which, though I fully appreciate their point of view, is a massive claim in view of the number of 'greats' who have worn the colours.

With his untiring energy allied to excellent ball control and passing ability, Colin could be part of the defence when needed, involved in the midfield or as an attacker – all in the space of time it took me to write this. In other words, 4-2-4 was just what it always is in top teams, a few numbers adding up to 10. Ignoring the poor goalkeeper, who could, like Liverpool's Tommy Lawrence, become assistant centre-halve when cracks appeared in the outfield defence, giving a back line of six or maybe more if panic had really set in!

Put a formation on that you number crunchers!

Colin was not the only exceptional talent in the evolving team at Maine Road, then City's ground. Up front there was a human dynamo in the stocky, blonde-haired figure of Francis Lee, so successful in business when he finished with football that he rose to be chairman of his old club. Signed from Bolton Wanderers for a then club record fee of £60,000 he slotted in at City as if it was exactly the job that had been waiting for him. I'd visit him at his home just outside Manchester and the talk would be of football – for a time. Then we'd broaden out into business chat.

Had I heard this, had I heard that . . . the questions kept coming, including "Your firm will have reel ends won't they?" (the last piece of paper left on a reel after our publications had been printed and the Presses were silent.) This question arose because Francis had involved himself in a factory which produced all sorts of paper products.

Happened I knew enough about the printing process to say "yes."

"Get me a chat with your manager, then. Maybe I can organise buying up the reel ends."

It happened that our manager, Andy Wilson, was a Manchester City supporter, so he was very willing to have the chat – and did.

Not that Francis got his wish. Apparently our reel ends were already contracted to go elsewhere, but it showed the Lee mind-set to be looking beyond his football career. So many players, who, in the days of wages a fraction of what they are today, made no plans for their future and suffered for it when the boots were hung up for the last time. The fact he became a millionaire when he finished with the game surprised me not one little bit.

What his business acumen didn't do while he was with City was interfere with his play. He was outside right with Bolton, but Allison in particular saw more in him that that. This was because there was another (originally) outside right brought in from Swindon Town for £35,000 – Mike Summerbee.

Mike was never short of a few hundred words or so on any subject and I loved his chat in his West Country accent (I enjoy accents of any description whether they be from Lands End or John o' Groats or anywhere in between). The only thing that surprised me was that the accent came from a young man born in Preston, in the north-west of England. Maybe his six years at Swindon Town was the answer.

I've mentioned before wingers who could sort out full backs if they tried to intimidate. Mike was a perfect example of this and woe-betide any defender who tried the 'hard man' stuff on him. I say defender rather than full back because the Summerbee-Lee pairing could switch from wing to centre-forward effortlessly and be just as effective through the middle or wide right. Both were fast, both were strong and although Mike's 47 goals scored in 375 games for City may seem paltry compared to Lee's 234 in 469, his list of 'assists' with the final pass or his physical ability to open up defences made him a constant danger to the opposition.

And there was one more essential cog in the City machine – Tony Book. If you went to a club and said you had a great player to offer them, saying "he's now 31, among his clubs have been Peasdown Miners, the Royal Army Medical Corps, Frome Town, Bath City, Toronto City and Plymouth Argyle," what do you think the reaction would be?

That's right – a question over your sanity. But that's exactly what Book's background was when he signed for City. And the reason was that Malcolm Allison knew exactly the full back's true qualities because he had signed him for Bath and Plymouth and was rightly convinced that, what others had missed could be to City's benefit.

Manager Mercer was not easy to convince. It took weeks and a few thousand words for Malcolm to persuade the man who made the transfer decisions, along with the directors, to spend what even then, was the paltry sum of £17,000 on the lean, sharp featured, not-too-athletic looking player who was already, by football standards, a veteran.

It was a long time ago, but the total transfer cost was roughly 10 per cent of what a top Premier League player earns IN A WEEK today and few, if any, will have a record as outstanding as his.

I remember Joe saying to me later, "I don't think Malcolm ever made out as strong a case for a player as for this one . . . and I sometimes wonder how I'd have felt if I'd stuck to my first reaction that he was too old and didn't have great pedigree."

"Gutted," would be my answer because of all the great signings, Tony Book turned out to be possibly the best taking it on a £ for £ basis.

Within weeks Joe realised that they had signed an extra special player – not only for his ability at full back, but for his authority and ability to lead. Tony was appointed captain and went on to play 244 games for City and captain them to all the successes of the Mercer-Allison regime. Later he even became manager and is as revered among the City faithful as the great Summerbee-Bell-Lee trio.

Yes, a great team which included these four when winning the Second Division and First Division titles, the FA Cup, the League Cup and the European Cup Winners Cup between 1965 and 1971; not forgetting such as Harry Dowd, Joe Corrigan, Glyn Pardoe, the almost constant half-back line of Doyle, Booth and Oakes, plus Neil Young and Coleman.

Back to the secret of the manager-coach success. Possibly a sort of good-cop, bad-cop approach. Malcolm didn't hesitate to handout criticism as the coach, Joe, in his office, would calm down angry players.

One such was Neil Young, transformed from leggy outside-left to a striker who totted up an impressive number of goals. He took a lot of stick from Allison after games and on the training ground and stormed in to see the manager about it. Joe listened patiently to the complaint then issued his advice.

"Go out there and show him how good you are," he said. "Play well, score goals – not that you are doing too badly – and that will shut him up."

So Young channelled his energies exactly the way the manager and coach wanted and moved his performances up several notches, including scoring the goal that won City the FA Cup against Leicester City and two in the defeat of Newcastle United which clinched the First Division title. It's called psychology by some. My description is 'common sense' and there was plenty of that from the two at the top.

Sadly for City as time progressed, Malcolm felt he wasn't getting enough praise for his contribution to the success. The pairing split and City have never reached the same heights again until new owners arrived and spent tens of millions on players – only a handful of them British.

My old friend Peter Gardener, sports writer with the *Manchester Evening News* once said of Neil Young, "When he plays well, City play well." and exactly the same was said about another player in Manchester, Pat Crerand, right-half with Manchester United. We first met when he was an up-and-coming reserve with Glasgow Celtic and I recall a chat with him and his young reserve team-mate Billy McNeil outside Celtic Park when they both made out a case for being promoted to the first team.

It happened when Jock Stein started building the team which was the first in Britain to win the European Cup and Billy went on to become a legend as captain of that team, aptly nicknamed the Lisbon Lions for their heroics in the Portuguese capital against much-fancied Inter Milan. But Crerand wasn't there on that memorable night. He had moved on to Manchester United, where Matt Busby told me, "We needed someone to produce the passes for our forwards and I decided he was the one."

Because the magnificent Bobby Murdoch was forcing his way through with Celtic, Stein reluctantly decided to let Crerand leave for £60,000. He did exactly what Busby signed him for, produced the passes which let the fearsome forwards George Best, Bobby Charlton and Denis Law lacerate opposing defences.

Not that everyone thought Crerand was all that good. Too slow, was the criticism levelled. So I put it to him, taking the risk that even though we knew one another well he would not take kindly to that criticism. In fact he quietly asked me, "Tell you what, they say I'm slow. You test that; how fast does the ball travel, from the time I get it until the player I send it to has it? I run ten yards and pass 30-35 yards. Other players run 30-35 and pass ten. It's the ball that counts. I'll bet I make it move faster than anyone."

I watched for this game after game and he was right. Perhaps he wasn't a greyhound but his through-the-eye-of-a-needle passes saw the ball move faster from point to point than anyone.

Chapter Fourteen

Ramsay 'Lift' Pays Off

'Right place at the right time', is one of the most quoted sayings in the English language and it certainly worked for me in Manchester. I had gone uptown to the Midland Hotel to see who was around. There was a European game in Liverpool that night and usually on those occasions, a gaggle (is that the right word) of football folk – managers, coaches, directors and a scattering of others had the habit of dropping into the Midland to see if they could learn anything about players, transfers or whatever before setting off for Liverpool.

There was a bit of a commotion going on as I talked to Dave Sexton, then manager of Chelsea. Naturally, I asked what was happening.

"Alf Ramsey's transport hasn't arrived or it's broken down and he was wanting to be off sharpish," he said.

On the right place, right time basis I excused myself and went to speak to the England manager who was sitting quietly in a corner. He was said to treat everyone with suspicion and Scotsmen with a considerable amount of dislike. I had heard these things about him but as I had never met him, didn't really know whether they were true or untrue. So I used the 'nothing ventured, nothing gained' approach. When I said who I was by way of starting the conversation, he accepted my handshake.

"Could I," I asked, "help by giving you a lift to Liverpool, as I'm leaving right now?"

It has since been suggested that I took my life in my hands trying this, but he couldn't have been more pleasant.

"Good," he said, rising from his seat and calling over a young Football Association official who was accompanying him. "We're off now."

The lad didn't get past "But . . . " before we were heading out the door and into my car. It would be great to say that the journey – because of heavy traffic it lasted an hour – was one long session of exclusive stories delivered by the England manager to a journalist doing him a favour, but I learned gradually that wasn't his style. (when he was knighted I asked what I would call him now and his answer was "what did you call me before – other than an awkward b-s-a-d??" I answered "Alf" and the reply was "so carry on"

We did talk . . . about the weather, about the Morris 1000 we were using and about the traffic. But about football? Nothing. So did the lift pay off? Definitely.

It wasn't long after that I took a phone call in The Weekly News office. It was Alf. In his clipped way of speaking he told me I might be interested in the fact that he had decided that Manchester United wing-half Nobby Stiles was to be a key figure in the team he was creating for the World Cup of 1966. An absolute tiger on the park, Nobby was one of the most likeable men I met in 50 years contact with footballers.

A family man who lived on the south side of Manchester. His charming wife Kay, his sons and he were the perfect family unit. I was never made anything but welcome when I dropped in for a chat though I would have hated to face him as an opponent on the park, where, though he was no giant, he feared no one and would have tackled anyone opposing his club or country's team. This time, though, I wasn't there to talk about club football, but about England and the fact he was about to become a key figure in the team.

What Alf had made abundantly clear was that though I could follow up his tip-offs I was not to say it came from him, so Nobby and Kay's first reaction to my prediction was to laugh! How did I know? Who told me? Was I making up a story for my paper? All I could answer was that I had been picking up bits and pieces of information from all over and had decided "Stiles for England" was a good bet.

Nobby was not inexperienced. He had some Under-23 honours and had been mentioned as one of several players to take what was then called a wing-half slot for his country. But most commentators put him in the 'outside chance' category whereas I knew he was, if not a certainty, as near as you can be in football to first choice. And so it turned out.

In all Nobby won 28 caps for his country – 16 in the unforgettable and historic year of 1966, when England won the World Cup for the only time in football history, so far at any rate. And who was the icon which stays with all of us when we remember that famous Wembley occasion? Nobby Stiles, prancing about the field with the trophy, stockings down round his ankles, toothless and expressing the sheer joy of every one of his team-mates and countrymen in the process.

So Alf did repay me for that car journey, short and all that it was.

* * *

Who was the real Ramsey?

A man considered surly by many because he wouldn't talk freely as so many football people (with very little to say) do now? A man who didn't even consider a player worth talking about unless he was English? A man who hated Scots?

These were among the views of many – especially Football Association big-wigs, who were happy to swan about the world with England and fawn over their manager while saying far from nice things behind his back. I recall one particular individual, who I had heard telling Alf how much he admired his training methods and discipline one minute, saying to me within the hour that "I wouldn't let him in the door of my club . . . it's time we changed managers ."

Alf had been less than a year in the job, the World Cup win was in the future. And when that happened? The same back-stabber was trying to tell me how it was the players who did the job, "Any manager could have won it with that squad" – while heading towards getting more than slightly inebriated on celebratory champagne.

Indeed, with Alf, it was 'who needs enemies with friends like that!' He didn't talk freely; he was only really at home with football folk – distrusting people in my job only a fraction less than the sycophants who clustered round him in the good times. But as a football writer who travelled around a fair bit with him I had no complaints. If I asked him a sensible question he gave me a sensible answer and that is a lot better than having someone with little to say thrashing on verbally as if he had.

Didn't consider a player talking about unless he was English? I honestly thought that was the case for a long time. Then, when I met him, amazingly, in my home town of Elgin when he was on a lecture tour and no longer managing , we had a chat. Some of it was about times gone by, but not all. I took the chance to mention his alleged totally English viewpoint about players and the answer was one I wish he had given some years before.

"You all believed I was interested only in English players," he said. "I had to be, but don't think for a minute I wouldn't have had Denis Law and George Best in my team."

"Any more?" I chanced.

Back into the shell, "Maybe, but not for now."

His alleged hatred of Scotsmen was built on a story, probably apocryphal, but claimed to have been overheard by many Glasgow journalists, that on arrival at Glasgow Airport for a game he was greeted with "Welcome to Scotland," and replied "That'll be f.....g right."

Did he say, didn't he? I don't know but I DO know that to this Scotsman he was almost never anything other than polite and, though never over-warm and friendly at least approachable.

Almost? I didn't worship at his shrine and therefore get a biased view of him and that was clear when I was with England in Brazil. I met up with Francis Lee, then with Manchester City and a forward of pace, power and ability, in the foyer of the team's hotel in Rio di Janeiro and we started chatting. Hardly had we begun than Alf was in about us. What did I think I was doing speaking to one of his players without first asking his permission?

Shades of Motherwell manager Bobby Ancell losing his temper with me 15 years before when I had visited Ian St John and his wife in their home, because Ian had invited me to come along for a chat. I was as angry with Alf as I had been with Bobby and began, "I've known Francis for years and I visit him regularly . . . " Which was where the player stepped in, verbally.

He pointed out that I did in fact visit him regularly in his home, by memory in Westhoughton, outside Manchester and that he trusted me and would carry on talking to me if he felt like it whatever Alf said. Unlike so many players he never backed down whether it was a full back or anyone else facing him. Alf turned on his heel without a word, never mentioned the incident again and equally, never changed his attitude to me or Lee, who, in the end, won 27 caps for England.

Oh and Lee and I chatted on and I ended up with a good story for *The Weekly News.*

I've made it clear all along that it was obvious to those as close up as I was to Alf that he was no admirer of officialdom as represented by club directors with positions in the Football Association hierarchy. It was never anything he said publicly, but his whole attitude when having to be in contact with those men was of impatience, of wishing he was somewhere else. And this was never better illustrated than on the night England won the world Cup.

I was in the same hotel as the entire England party – the Royal Garden, Kensington. It was a beautiful hotel with a balcony above the entrance where the players, who had just achieved football's highest honour for their country, went out to wave to the supporters who were exulting in the glory of it all. My room overlooked the balcony and the crowds, roaring their appreciation, waving Union Jack flags and using car horns to spell out da-da, da-da-da, da-da-da-da-da . . . ENGLAND. Even as a Scot, I could feel the emotion of it all, as did my fellow onlookers, Dennis Lowe, from Manchester, and senior Sunday Post columnist Jack Harkness.

But important events were in the offing and though the crowds stayed on, the players, manager and coaching staff went back to their rooms to prepare for the official banquet, now, of course, a celebratory affair. Having helped with the Sunday Post coverage of the final, my job was seemingly over for the day, so, as I had booked to stay until the next day before returning to Manchester, I envisaged a meal, a quiet drink and an early night.

After the first two, I decided, as a last round-up, to go downstairs to see if there was anything happening around the dinner. As I strolled along the corridor I could see two women chatting and when they turned to see who was coming I recognised Kay Stiles and Tina Moore, wives of Nobby Stiles and team captain Bobby Moore. Thinking they were probably having a break from the meal, I asked if they were enjoying themselves.

"Not us," said Tina, "The Football Association didn't invite wives to join their husbands in there!"

Used as I was by this time to the blundering of officialdom, I honestly wasn't too surprised.

Tina went on, "But Alf is going to be leading the players out soon and wives and girlfriends will join them for a night on the town."

Here I was, the last reporter standing (and that was true in the sense that most of my English colleagues and many others were well into their umpteenth celebratory drink by then) with the final story of the day – and only a Scottish-based Sunday newspaper, with its English edition long gone, to send it to.

The ladies and I chatted for a few minutes more, then Alf lead the players out, long before officialdom had intended but 100 per cent understandable in the circumstances. I headed off for a telephone as the now 'joined up' party headed for their night out; which is why news of the mess-up appeared first in a newspaper printed some 400 miles for the source.

What was that I said earlier about 'right place, right time?'

Chapter Fifteen

England's World Cup 1966

When the name of Alf Ramsey crops up there is always the same statement made, mostly by people who don't study the situation fully enough, or go on hearsay. It is that he was the man who saw the end of wingers in the game.

I was on England's the pre-World Cup 1966 tour of Finland, Norway, Denmark and Poland and the Ramsey squad included wingers of genuine talent in Ian Callaghan (Liverpool), Peter Thompson (Liverpool) and Terry Paine (Southampton). All are still revered as players in the cities in which they were based and rightly so. They could take on defenders of all shapes and sizes and by dint of skill and pace get beyond them.

But there lay the flaw in the England manager's opinion. Their talent was in going forward, the talent in fact of all wingers of their day and forever previously. Wingers stayed wide and up-field, passes were delivered to them and they took on the opposing full back.

Alf Ramsey was the first to see their job differently. He wanted men who would use the wide areas of the field in an attacking sense, but would spring into those areas from deeper, from around where half-backs (midfield players) usually operated. These men would not only have attacking duties, they would also have a non-stop work ethic which meant they would also have passing duties, defensive responsibility and the job of attacking like wingers! It was a tall order, but he had in his sights two men perfectly suited for the task in West Ham's Martin Peters and the inimitable, irrepressible Alan Ball.

If Ball ever stood still on a football field I can't recall it. He was always working, always chirping away at others in his high-pitched voice, a dynamo with Blackpool, with Everton, with Arsenal and others. He was the youngest in the World Cup winning team, but you would never have known it because of his confidence in himself and his pride in wearing the white shirt which never diminished after a total of 72 caps.

It might be said that Peters was the opposite, relatively quiet, not appearing to be forever working, but, in fact, he had only one drawback. For some strange reason Ramsey described him as "Ten years ahead of his time." In many ways, with wingers on the way out, he was, but those sort of tags give cynics the opportunity to criticise. Peters was a key man in all of his 67 appearances for his country.

Like it or lump it – and especially in the early stages a huge number of people lumped it – the new system worked because of the manager's belief in it and the effort put in by the players to make it work. Mind you he didn't half have a plus with the players he finally settled on. The only major omission, raising eyebrows among the fans was that of Jimmy Greaves, the Chelsea and Spurs goal machine, who took it badly. In a similar situation to that of wingers, Ramsey looked on Greaves at not ticking ALL the boxes. Lacking mostly was working backwards, getting into the grafting side of the game in midfield and even deeper in emergencies.

Jimmy was a scorer, more than a poacher, less than a physical presence and non-stop grafter. Absolutely nothing wrong with that for the vast majority of people, but Ramsey wanted more, big strong men either side of the world-class distributor and scorer Bobby Charlton.

And he got it in West Ham's Geoff Hurst, hat-trick hero of the final against West Germany and the much under-estimated Roger Hunt, of Liverpool, who could score too and never stopped working.

When players like that are backed by my equal favourite goalkeeper of all time, Gordon Banks (he rates with me along with Peter Schmeichel of Manchester United around 30 years later) full backs George Cohen (Fulham) fast and effective and Ray Wilson (Everton) a classic left-footed left back. Add the already mentioned Nobby Stiles, an English Colossus to equal Bill Shankly's favourite Ron Yeats. Jack Charlton, brother of Bobby, as outgoing in public as Bobby was reserved, and the inimitable captain, Bobby Moore, second to none in football history as a reader of the game and anticipator of opposition moves, then you have a formidable team.

Lucky to win the World Cup because – it was in England – because the Argentine captain was sent off in a tense game – because there was a 'goal that never was' in the final?

As a Scot, I am supposed to answer "YES," but I'm afraid I can't since as a football writer for many years and someone who was really close up to the game, I can't recall any successful team, at club or international level, not having a fair proportion of luck on their way to winning a trophy. And I will add that every football-loving fellow Scot would be absolutely delighted if our national team could get a large dollop of luck every time WE enter a European or World cup tournament.

Which really brings me to my next football 'life', but, not before I round off my English experience, with some 'snapshot' thoughts . . .

I had the pleasure of the friendship of Denis Law and his charming wife Diane. Most of the chats with them were in their house on the fringe of Manchester – and I have never known anyone drink so many cups of tea as Denis.

We'd start chatting over our first cup. Not long after the second cup would be on offer. Any reasonable length of chat and a third and fourth cup would be drunk all from fresh pots brewed by the player who could have had any number of people delighted to do the job for him – which was when I usually realised I had at least a 45 minute drive home on a good day, along traffic jammed streets where toilets were none too plentiful. Actually, I had no accidents, but there were times when I came close!

Denis was, of course, from Aberdeen and as my home town was Elgin, we had an original accent in common, though, because he'd joined Huddersfield Town as a 14 year old, his was a strange mix.

I recall a piece of graffiti in my home area of Chorlton-cum-Hardy, where Denis, Diane and family had lived for a spell which to me, summed up what Manchester United supporters – and many in the wider football world – thought of him.

Sprayed first on the wall of a railway bridge were the words 'Bobby Charlton King'.

That survived alone for a brief spell – until, in larger letters, appeared the phrase 'Denis Law – GOD'.

I was fortunate to be in England when some of the greatest managers of all time were in charge of clubs, but all the top bosses weren't with the big outfits.

I think particularly of people like JIMMY SIRREL (Notts County), TED BATES (Southampton), HARRY POTTS (Burnley). Jimmy would have made the impact of a Shankly had he bossed at Liverpool. His pawky Glasgow humour hid a football brain second to none. Harry, like so many managers of the time, never really trusted 'the Press' but he built a team good enough to have us returning to Turf Moor regularly to watch a skilled and attractive outfit.

We were not always welcome. In fact for a spell there was a tie doing the rounds among the football writers in the north-west which read 'Banned by Burnley'. It was the result of a ban imposed by chairman BOB LORD. A butcher and a man who fell out with many people regularly, he decided that 'the Press' treated his club with less respect than say, Manchester United and the other city giants.

However, Bob did have someone who could keep him in his place – his wife! I know this because of a train journey from Glasgow to Preston after a League game between Scotland and England. After a couple of interviews with players I couldn't find a seat on the crowded train – until I spotted one in the official Football League compartment.

I opened the door and was immediately told by Mr Lord – "No Press in here . . . find another seat." Just as I was about to enter into an argument, another voice interrupted.

"Nonsense, you can come and sit by me," said Mrs Lord. "Move up Bob."

I had met Mrs Lord at Turf Moor on a match day and we had chatted amicably. I always remember her as a neatly dressed woman who wore a black 'choker' round her neck and on this occasion I was very grateful to her as many passengers had to stand all the way to Preston.

Also in the carriage was ALAN HARDAKER, secretary of the Football League, and without doubt one of the most powerful and influential men ever to hold an official position in English football. I visited him in his Lytham St Anne's headquarters regularly and though he seldom gave a direct story he would guide me to one or more, usually provided by his assistant ERIC HOWARTH, a superb organiser who never sought the limelight but deserved to be in it.

What Hardaker made clear throughout his time as secretary was his dislike of 'big clubs like Manchester United trying to run the game', as he put it. It led to many tense discussions between him and the Matt Busby's of the football world, but during his time, the game was a much more level playing field than it has become.

Maybe he wouldn't have been able to stop the ludicrous wage explosion for players or other ills that affected the game after he had gone but rest assured, he would have tried and I also doubt if television would have had the suffocating influence it has on the game today.

Chapter Sixteen

Back to Dundee

Our time in England had been mostly a pleasant experience because of many friendships formed, in my case in the football world and in the case of the family with people from all walks of life. Our children stayed on south of the Border, daughter Laura in York, son Graeme in Manchester but it was very different for me on returning to our native country, first to *The Weekly News*, then as sports editor of the daily paper *The Courier*.

This was mostly down to the aggression of one man – Jim McLean, an inside forward with Ayr United when I left for England, manager of Dundee United when I returned. Let me make it clear that I cannot but praise him and his associates such as Walter Smith, later to manage Rangers (twice), Everton and Scotland; and the man who had been a goal-scoring machine in his days with Raith Rovers, Gordon Wallace and was now, like Smith, a coach. Between them they took a team that had been a joke when I departed Scotland into the highest echelons of Scottish and European football.

But, for some reason which he never explained, the relationship between McLean and me – to repeat a phrase used by Bill Shankly when his Liverpool team lost a game against much inferior opposition – "Started badly and fell away!" But let's get things in perspective. One of the most fraught of all occupations is football club management. You have to please directors, supporters, and the media not to mention getting a team of temperamentally different players to do what you want – which is winning every game.

The mental pressure is enormous because you know that at some point or other in any season – or even close season for that matter – you will fall foul of one or other, or some, or all of those groups. The players can be happy with you but the directors think you are too uppity and cocky for their liking because you have won a game or two – or did you have to pay all that money (which they look on as their property) for that player you said was perfect and, so far, isn't?

The players take a dislike to you because one of them, well liked by the rest, has been left out of the team or told off for only (?) having a few drinks too many. Maybe you used to play against them in your active days and did or said something they didn't like. Footballers have long memories.

And the supporters? There's a laugh. Some actually do support you through thick or thin, but others, to use the old story, don't have much of a life at home. They take it out on the manager, players, directors, groundsmen, physiotherapists, trainers (one or other or the lot) on match days and nights.

Summing it up, a manager might have the support of his wife (not always) and pals (including 'crawlers' intent on getting free tickets) but other than that, he is isolated. So perhaps, edginess, short temper and mood swings are inevitable.

Even that master of cool, Matt Busby, was seen to exhibit facial traces of annoyance, express himself forcibly in the privacy of the dressing room or his office or send heavier than normal pipe smoke trails skywards on occasion when things weren't going the way he wanted. So I will leave others to judge why the Dundee United manager sometimes behaved as if he had a tree, never mind a chip, on his shoulder – and not just towards me. He banned me four times – or maybe it was five – in my ten years as sports editor of the Dundee-based daily paper. I believe others suffered the same fate on occasion, but my experience is enough for me.

However, McLean, with the help of an outstanding coaching staff, took a rubbish team which had been moulded into a good team by his predecessor Gerry Kerr, up another notch which brought them big attendances, League and League Cup titles and deep respect in Europe where they were finalists in the UEFA Cup. So the fact he and I weren't pals doesn't really matter in the bigger scheme of things.

That was one of the few flies in the ointment on my return. Many of the friends I had known as players were now either in the veteran stage, had moved up to coaching, managing, scouting or doing anything to keep them in touch with football. Some had even moved out of the game – mostly reluctantly.

The balance at club level had completely changed in the 17 years or so I'd been away. In Dundee alone, the power base had reversed itself. Dundee, the BIG club, the championship and Cup-winning outfit of my early days when George Anderson, Billy Steel, Bob Shankly, Alan Gilzean and others successfully ruled the roost were now also-rans compared with the formerly joke club Dundee United.

This was first of all down to a shrewd, pipe smoking manager of the old school, Gerry Kerr. The former Rangers player had quietly gone about the business of building a team including Scandinavian players and behind this had recruited young players from the area around Dundee.

Eventually though, he gave way to McLean, an inside forward I remembered from my earlier days in Scotland, and one of the three brothers – himself, Willie and Tommy, who was the most successful as a player and a winner of, among other honours, the European Cup Winners Cup with Rangers, where he was a quality winger.

Jim was a useful inside forward who read the game well and who also had played with Dundee, which didn't make his elevation to manager across the road at United, initially popular with supporters of the club. It wasn't long though before he won them over by building a team which brought league championship and League Cup success.

This was due to his ability to bring the best out of his players, and also to the remarkable fact that so many of the team hailed from no more than a decent bus ride from the club's Tannadice Park headquarters.

To this day, supporters can reel off their names – Hamish McAlpine, Billy Thomson, Richard Gough, Frank Kopel, Maurice Malpas, Billy Kirkwood, John Holt, Paul Hegarty, Dave Narey, Ralph Milne, Paul Sturrock, Davie Dodds, Eamonn Bannon and others less well publicised but who did a job when called upon.

I was happy to get back into Scottish football – for a time! In England I had moved out of the game for work inside our Manchester office, then had come the switch back to head office in Dundee. After a spell with *The Weekly News* I returned to the daily paper, *The Courier and Advertiser,* now simply *The Courier* – and to a job I came to dislike intensely, the inside part of being Sports Editor.

For large parts of my life I had dealt with the clatter of linotype machines and thunder of printing machines, hot metal and page lay-outs. All my life I had equally not thought of it as what I wanted, that being where things were happening, meeting people, getting stories, writing those stories then seeing them in print. I had respect for those who sub-edited incoming stories, applied headings and laid out pages, but to me the real work was that of the creator and writer.

Everyone all the way through to the street-corner newspaper seller: reporters, sub-editors, copy-takers on their typewriters, caseroom men, printers, advertising and circulation staff and all the rest – were and are important. Before the advent of computers, copy-takers could 'find' a reporter on the telephone no matter which part of the world he was in and cheerily pass on news from home while typing at an amazing speed the proffered story. My (admittedly biased) view was and still is that none of them would be there if first someone didn't get the stories which filled the pages.

For nearly two years I worked hard on the 'inside' job, even though I didn't like it. This was especially true because *The Courier* was a broadsheet and I had been used, for nearly 30 years, to working on the tabloid sized *Weekly News* and *Sunday Post*. Lay-out techniques in particular are frustratingly different in both and a different style of sub-editing and applying headlines also comes into the reckoning.

If you are a 'half-full' kind of a person, as I am, as opposed to a 'half-empty' pessimist, you always believe in silver linings. Mine came in the shape of friend, colleague and former top class player with Dundee, Tommy Gallacher, then chief football writer with *The Courier*. Due to cover the 1982 World Cup in Spain with Scotland – those were the days when Scotland regularly qualified for the major football tournament – Tommy took ill.

Called in to editor Ian Stewart's office, I was asked if I would be prepared to take Tommy's place as I had previous experience of the

World Cup with England and had travelled widely from both Glasgow and Manchester offices. I was slow saying "yes" – well relatively so. It was all of three or four seconds before I did!

And that began the final eight or nine years of my career as a football writer.

Trouble was that the 'call' came so late that the World Cup in Spain, after the Scotland party had prepared in Portugal, was almost on us and there wasn't time to change the accreditation from Tommy's name to mine, but I wasn't going to let a detail like that stand in the way of getting back 'on the road' as it were.

So off went Ian Wheeler with Tommy Gallacher's credentials; and the first obstacle was entering Portugal. Fortunately Tommy's passport picture was not unlike me – dark-haired and vaguely similar facially – and there was a crowd of Scots in the party all clamouring to get to their hotel and on to the phone. So the glance at the passport was brief to say the least and no questions were asked. Much the same thing happened when we moved on to Spain, but a sterner test was ahead . . . accreditation for the actual World Cup tournament.

Here, I got lucky. I had to report to a young woman, incidentally with the reddest hair and greenest eyes I had ever seen, which is anything but the colouring you expect to see in a Spanish girl. Fortunately she was an avid football fan and almost immediately asked if I could get her the autographs of the Scotland players and officials. Of course I said "yes" then asked (she spoke perfect English) if I could explain an accreditation problem I had to her. I presented the 'pre-accreditation' data I had (in Tommy's name) and told her the full story of the late switch. She listened carefully to what I had to say, asked me to stand aside for a moment or two, and lifted a phone on her desk.

As the moment or two became minutes and she looked quite solemn as she spoke and listened, I began to think things were going against me. When she finally finished she beckoned me back to the desk. It was a difficult situation, she said, but a letter I had from the editor Ian Stewart explaining it, my passport and my official DC Thomson Press card had been accepted as proof I was who I said I was and was telling the truth. Apparently there were two other instances of late changes but all three had proved to be genuine. So I got my accreditation, in my own name . . . oh! and she got her autographs as she was in the Press centre later, working on statistics and I was able to hand them over.

* * *

So I was 'back on the road' and working as a reporter. However, a couple of decades had passed and it was not like the days when I had been centred in Glasgow. It was wonderful to be where the best teams were, the east coast Dundee (United) and Aberdeen, but the rest of Scottish football had definitely suffered a steep decline. No longer were there outstanding players sprinkled through the game with clubs like East Fife, Raith Rovers, Falkirk, Clyde and so on. Crowds watching clubs other than Rangers and Celtic (apart again from the New Firm of Dundee United and Aberdeen) were steadily getting smaller.

If I hadn't previously been involved in Scottish football I might not have noticed these changes gradually showing, but I had something to compare with and they were comparisons which disappointed me. I was again lucky enough to be where things were definitely looking up.

Relations between the press and the managers of Dundee and Aberdeen continued to be strained and I felt that they did not understand the role of the reporter in providing honest comment and impartial assessment rather than merely acting as a spin doctor. We prided ourselves just as much as being an expert in our walk of life as they in theirs.

It led, as mentioned earlier, to pathetic 'bans' from the clubs, in my case four or five over a ten year period by McLean which certainly did the club no good and over which I didn't lose any sleep since I knew he would have to give in after a spell. The longest lasted six weeks – at a time when nothing special was happening to the club anyway, so the effect was zero.

What were they for? In one case it was over the transfer of a player. McLean claimed he had paid a certain fee; I checked with the manager of the selling club and got a totally different figure. I mentioned there was a difference of opinion and the next time I visited the club to speak to him he was apoplectic and ordered me "never to darken our doorstep again" – or words to that effect, in what is called in some quarters 'industrial language'.

Fortunately, certainly in the case of United, the players I had to deal with were as friendly as their manager wasn't! And top level players they were. I have already named them, but I would like to pay particular attention to a few.

Two of the best midfield players (wing-halves in my parlance) ever to come out of Scottish football were Dundee based. I have already expressed my admiration for Doug Cowie, the Dundee player of over 20 years earlier. His counterpart now was David Narey (they had 55 Scotland caps between them, which should and would have been more like 155 had they featured with either of the big Glasgow clubs) whose partnership with team captain Paul Hegarty at the centre of defence was a major part of the reason why United won the league and League Cups.

I doubt if you could meet anyone in football as self-effacing as Narey, yet his record of 578 games for United in domestic competition and in 75 Europe (which remained a record for a Scottish player for 16 years) proves his quality and the wonderful reputation United have in Europe. He trained hard, went home, played magnificently in game after game for United and Scotland (35 caps) but was happy to stay out of the headlines – except, for example, when a loud-mouthed Englishman of my acquaintance put him there.

In the 1982 World Cup in Seville, Spain, playing against Brazil – whose football writers, the most critical in the world, made it clear to me how highly they rated him ("He could be Brazilian," said one) – Dave scored the opening goal from 25 yards. As the stadium rose to him and everyone acknowledged the quality of the shot, my English friend from the time when the manager of Coventry City, Jimmy Hill, described it as "a toe poke."

Never high in Scotland, Jimmy's reputation as a commentator plummeted to new depths after this piece of stupidity and never recovered. All I did was to regret his comment because I liked him as a person, while accepting his 'over-the-top' style of attracting attention. It had worked when he pulled Coventry up to respectability in English football, but kept going 'way out of line' as a football commentator.

The Narey reaction? A shoulder shrug and "Well that's what he thinks." I've known players who would have gone looking for Jimmy intent on causing him physical damage, but that, or any other form of confrontation, just wasn't the Narey way.

I recall one of many other occasions when his self-effacement surfaced. We were in Mexico for the World Cup of 1986 and the Scotland players had been booked into isolated accommodation which was, 'doing our heads in' according to one of the less reticent members of the party. He who put it this way, "Why did Ernie Walker (the then Scottish Football Association secretary) put us in this dump. Is he punishing us for what happened back in 1978?" (of that, more later).

Looking for The Courier angle, I came across Narey quietly reading in a corner of the lounge. Before I got in a question he asked "Been in touch with home?".

Sending daily reports I obviously had. "So what's the weather like?" he asked and I told him.

"Any other news?" was the next query and, as I had a few snippets from conversation with colleagues back home I passed them on.

And so it went on until I had to stop him and point out in the friendliest way that I was here to ask him questions, not the other way round.

"Sorry," he said, "gets a bit boring here," before giving me a few quotes.

He was obviously homesick, but, typically, knew that his day job was football, knew he had to travel, did that, worked hard and played hard.

Which brings us to Hegarty. Bought as a centre-forward from Hamilton Accies and converted, despite being on the small side for the position, to centre-half by McLean, he was a tad more communicative than his partner, but not much. I put that down to the McLean habit of making his displeasure felt if a player did anything he didn't approve of, including saying something to The Press.

There were those on the staff who didn't worry too much – like Narey, Richard Gough, centre-half, Hamish McAlpine, sent home from Japan on one occasion for allegedly stepping out of line and Mr Perpetual Motion himself, Eamonn Bannon, who adopted the principle of ignoring any McLean outbursts and getting on with the game. The rest weren't frightened of their manager, they just preferred to avoid his rants by being careful what they said.

Hegarty's position was different. He was the skipper and his opinion was sought by reporters more often than others. Admirably he managed the difficult task of giving quotes, but not being stupid. Then if McLean didn't approve, he fought his corner very well indeed.

Others easy to remember included Paul Sturrock, who adopted the dangerous habit, especially for a centre-forward, of playing with his stockings rolled down to his ankles. How good was he? Let's put it this way – he seldom missed a game because of leg damage because he was a master of not being where defenders thought he was when they lunged in for the ball. His style of play was arrogant, but when you are as skilful as he was you are entitled to a fair share of that commodity.

Best example of this was when United put Barcelona out of Europe – again. To get the background here; Barcelona were giants in the world of football. Dundee United, relatively small-time by comparison and Barca were, at the time managed by an Englishman, Terry Venables, and had as regular first-team players Gary Lineker and Mark Hughes.

When I interviewed them in the hotel in St Andrews where they stayed prior to their game at United's Tannadice Park, I classed Venables whom I had seen play and met as a manager in England, as trying hard to give the impression that he rated United, but was in fact already looking to the next round; Lineker as conscious of his unquestioned ability as a goal scorer and perhaps not too happy about this fixture away from the big club, big city atmosphere and Hughes as thoroughly likeable person with a load of ability and respect for any and every team he faced. Right or wrong? Just my opinion . . .

But back to Sturrock. Over both games, which United won with surprising ease, he was magnificent with the highlight coming in

Barcelona. I suffer from vertigo and the Press box at the magnificent Nou Camp stadium, where the trophy room alone is awe-inspiring, is perched so high that I couldn't look what felt like straight down on the near touch-line. Suddenly, from that touch-line area Sturrock appeared, ball at his feet and walking rather than running with it. The stockings were down as usual, the shorts almost indecently short as he strolled along, completely unmarked because, like he did so often he had 'lost' his marker. Then, a few yards from the touchline, he calmly cut the ball back for the incoming defender, John Clark, to blast into the net – score Barcelona 1, United 2 . . . game over, Dundee United humbling Barcelona for the fourth time in the UEFA Cup.

As a final Barca memory, there was the Kevin Gallacher goal in Dundee. Kevin, nephew of Tommy Gallacher and a lightning fast outside right, was causing the Catalan giants all sorts of problems. But when he got the ball nearer the halfway line than the bye-line, there seemed no danger. A few steps forward and he sent over a cross . . . or was it?

It certainly looked like that to me and when the ball looped its way into the net for a goal, there was a distinct pause in the Press box before we realised what had happened.

Kevin naturally, claimed he meant it as a goal scoring attempt and I am the last person in the world to say he is wrong to make that claim. But it will forever be in my memory as a cross which miraculously did something in the air and became a goal!

Kevin went on to play for Coventry City, Blackburn Rovers, Newcastle United, Preston North End, Sheffield Wednesday and Huddersfield Town in a career which ended after 431 club games and 53 appearances for Scotland. But for several serious injuries, that would have been an even more impressive CV, but my outstanding memory of him will always be that goal against Barcelona.

* * *

It may look from this as if all I did was to get involved with Dundee United. Nothing could be further from the truth and their near neighbours

Dundee FC (the two grounds, Tannadice and Dens Park, are the closest together of any major clubs in Britain) won the League Cup the year I returned to Scotland. They were runners-up in Division 1 the same year.

However, things then went pear-shaped. Managers came and went, not all of them because of lack of ability, but often because of Board Room whims and fancies; chairmen and players seemed to have the same revolving door tendency. It came to the stage that, when a call came from Dens Park about a Press conference, it was difficult to work out whether it would be a transfer, a managerial sacking or appointment or a change of chairman.

Shades of my earlier association with the club . . . the wonderful George Anderson era, the Bob Shankly era, Billy Steel, Doug Cowie, Alan Gilzean and so on. That stability, those successes, were consigned to history and the reminiscences of older supporters.

To me the most memorable chairman was a Canadian (though there is some doubt about that) Ron Dixon. He breezed into Dens exactly the time I and freelance football writer Dick Donnelly were leaving. As soon as we heard the accent, we about-turned and checked that he was in fact the new man in charge. Identities established on both sides, I asked what had tempted him to move into Scottish football.

The astounding reply was "The history of this club and the regular attendances of 35,000."

When Dick and I recovered, we asked him where he had heard that.

"From a source within the club," was the answer.

We pointed out that this sort of 'gate' had been back in the 1940s, 50s and 60s (the record was 43,000 for a Rangers game in 1953) and that 5000 to 10,000 was a more realistic figure now.

He simply refused to believe us until the last time I saw him before he became the ex-chairman – and disappeared out of our lives until a mysterious demise in Canada brought him back into the headlines – when he said "Maybe I should have believed you lads and done what you did that first day – about-turned!"

He definitely got that right.

Chapter Seventeen

The Optimistic World Cup

The other side of the job 'back home' was the international team.

In the years leading up to my retiral I reported on three World Cup tournaments – in Spain, Mexico and Italy. The euphoria of getting there gradually reduced to nothing by the inability to get further than the first round games.

The travelling supporters, the 'Tartan Army', enjoyed themselves all right. They hoped for great things but were mostly astute enough to know they weren't likely to happen, so looked on their journeys as wonderful foreign holidays to places they had always wanted to visit. Without, in most cases, families in tow, they were able to have 'lads fun' without restrictions – other than financial.

The really optimistic World Cup had been in Argentina in 1978. Team manager then was my old friend Ally McLeod. Such was his charisma he had the nation believing not only in the journey but in the final result – WINNING the Cup.

Cool, calm logic brought into the equation that there was no chance of this happening, but then if that was your thought process, you probably hadn't met Ally. This was a man with a style of belief in what he said which automatically had you believing in him and what he was putting forward. I knew this because of many chats with him in his very earliest footballing days – well chat implies a brief get-together, his were more full-blown briefings.

At the time, he was a part-time player with Third Lanark and I was working in Glasgow and on one particular occasion, standing on the edge of the Cathkin Park pitch, he held out his multi-coloured hands to me! The explanation of this rainbow effect was that he was in an apprenticeship in which he dealt with chemicals and those stained his hands.

"This isn't for me" he said, "Football is going to be my life and I'll be good enough to make it big in the game."

And he did. As a long-legged, awkward left winger for Third Lanark and Blackburn Rovers, where he edged towards becoming a midfield player (wing-half) who became just that for Hibs; then as a manager, particularly with Aberdeen, where he set up the club for a certain Alex Ferguson to build even further . . . into European Cup Winners cup winners.

Never underestimate what Ally gave to Scottish football. There are those who said he built up optimism so high before the 1978 World Cup that things were bound to go wrong. Rubbish! If the players he chose had played to their potential it is distinctly possible that Scotland, for once, would have qualified for the latter stages of the tournament. But he made the mistake of trusting them to dedicate themselves to the task in hand and they let him down.

The Scottish trait of underestimating opponents – Iran for one, with whom they drew 1-1, was down to the players. Instead of regarding their opponents a layer or two beneath them in international football as they did Holland (a 3-2 win) a layer or two above them, four days later, then all would have been well.

But a core of players decided it was summer and they were on holiday. A Scottish holiday for many consisting of doing little and drinking a lot. So the pre-World Cup dream of glory fizzled out into recriminations and the sending home of Willie Johnston for alleged drug misuse.

I sensed the next time I met Ally and in subsequent meetings, that the fire of ambition had been dimmed, the burning will to win, to be a success reduced to no more than embers. I am still proud that we were friends and just wish that things had panned out differently for a decent man and a definite personality in the world of football.

* * *

On a wall in all our houses since we married back in 1950 has been a picture. It is of a young lad lying on his back on a cliff-top obviously thinking of the future; places to go, people to meet, adventure. It doesn't look any like me, but it could be me – lying on top of the Daisy Rock in Hopeman, in my native county of Moray, having a rest after fishing from the rocks below and dreaming of the future. And high on the list of wishes was that I would visit two countries in particular . . . America and Brazil and two cities there in particular, LOS ANGELES and RIO de JANIERO. To me, the names alone were magic and even more magical was the fact that I achieved my ambition and visited them both thanks to football.

It was BRAZIL first, with England and en route MEXICO and URUGUAY. Like every child of the 1920s I grew up when the cinema was expanding, talkies had come in and flickering pictures had steadied and were watchable without eye strain. On a Saturday afternoon we could see the children's matinees in my home town of Elgin for 2d – that's less than 1 pence in today's currency, it was called the 'tuppeny rush.'

For that we got a short movie and the main feature – and any misbehaving was ended by the intervention of one of a team of girls with the principal duty of seeing everyone to their seats, but a secondary one of keeping order. They were backed by a uniformed man who scrutinised you with an eagle eye as you paid your money and took over as discipline supervisor when everyone was in and settled down. The favourite films fell into two categories – what we called cowboys and Indians and far-fetched it-will-never-happen (!!) space adventures.

But I digress. The 'baddies', if they weren't native American Indians or white men turned nasty, they were Mexican. Now I had grown up a long way from those days, but I didn't really know what to expect when I arrived in Guadalajara with the England party for the first time.

Mexico

I didn't expect what the early films called 'bandido's' but many areas of Mexico had an unhealthy reputation for drug problems and the attendant violence. Maybe I was lucky, but I saw none of it.

I'd had a series of vaccinations before heading west and was still a bit groggy when we arrived in Mexico, so that may account for my first experience – collapsing with heat-stroke, which in the end was down to my own stupidity.

"Even when you get used to it, remember that the sun at this time of the year (it was June) is much, much hotter than we are used to," said the doctor with the party.

So I carefully went under the shade of an umbrella to type my stories for *The Weekly News*. What I forgot was that the sun moves and shade moves with it. I suddenly felt hot and bothered, saw the faces of Geoffrey Green of *The Times*, Don Saunders of *The Telegraph* and others start to distort and woke up.

The bit in between apparently saw me slide off my chair unconscious and stay that way for five minutes or so until a splash of cold water to my face and a loosening of my collar brought me round. When I recovered I was able to get back to work – in the shade and keeping a close eye on the shadow.

Among other memories of Guadalajara is one of the best steak and chips I have ever enjoyed. Brian Glanville, the Times football writer at the time and a man of many languages, asked if I'd like to sample some local cooking instead of hotel food. I did – and off we went into town.

On a square, milling with local people, we came across what I can only describe as the biggest barbecue grill I have ever seen. On it steaks as big as soup plates and thick as your wrist were sizzling their way to perfection and, in a large metal bowl full of fat also being heated by the flames under the grill, huge potatoes had been cut in four and were browning beautifully. I love my steak and chips, but this was beyond anything I had ever experienced and taste. I can still recall it.

In fluent Spanish. Brian ordered for both of us. The man in charge, small, fat with a heavy, black moustache and, I am certain, an extra in my Mexican movies of earlier days, was immediately aware we were visitors and, after dishing out a huge plateful similar to those doing the rounds near us, added chips to the mound already there.

Did I finish the delicacy? Honestly no, which had nothing to do with quality, merely quantity, but it is undeniable that I did our host and his fare justice, as did Brian. After acclimatising in Guadalajara the party moved on to Mexico City for England's game against Mexico. Now that is a city!

"How many people live here?" I asked of a Mexican journalist. "No one really knows," he replied. I have since seen 15,000,000, 20,000,000 and more quoted, but it seems still no one knows for sure. As far as I am concerned that will apply forever because the population seems always to be swirling, coming and going, arriving and leaving.

It has, along with six-lane-each-way city highways, slums and grand houses, downtrodden peasants and high rollers, some marvellous city squares featuring tavernas, open air tables and chairs – and mariachi bands.

Work over for the day a group of journalists retired to a city square for a meal. Half-way through we were approached by a group of men bearing musical instruments, violins, trumpet, guitar and what I would term a mini-double bass and dressed in wide-brimmed Mexican hats and silver studded outfits which I later found were described as 'charro'. Could they play for us? Indeed they could as the night was warm, the food exactly to order and the mood relaxed with interviews, writing and telephoning behind us for the day.

I love music – not of the classic variety though I can appreciate some of that, but swing, jazz, rock 'n roll, country and western and more or less anything not based on twanging guitars belting out same again, same again, rhythm. And to that, from the moment they started up on that night in Mexico City, you can add MARIACHI. I was absolutely entranced by the wonderful melodies played by a line-up I had never seen before and which produced a sound unique in my experience.

Daily Mirror columnist Frank McGhee was obviously enjoying it just as much and when he suggested a whip round of pesos and the additional purchase of a crate of Mexican Cervesas (beer) for the players, coins and paper notes quickly piled up on the table. The beer had long gone before our Mariachi band left the scene with much doffing of sombreros and expressions of thanks.

Wonderful but not so wonderful though, a mix of funny and pathetic was an encounter with another type of person. Invited to a British Embassy reception – the Press Corps always were with England, but never, in my time, with Scotland – I went to join Brian Glanville, sitting on the steps of a stair. He was in conversation with a lady laden with expensive jewellery and sporting a cut-glass accent and they were talking about public schools. Suddenly the attention turned to me when Brian said, "of course Ian is also a public school boy," (as he had been). In the context of sensational claims that might seem very near the top of the list, but it was true.

"Which one was that," queried the grand dame.

Recovering from the seeming sudden elevation to higher education, dead-pan, I answered, "The East End public school, Elgin."

There was a pause and an uncertain, "Oh, I see."

What we had done, of course, was tell the truth, but about two totally different establishments. In England a public school is what we in Scotland would call a private school. In Scotland a public school is where everyone, from the time their education starts, attends. So we had both, in fact, been public school boys.

By the looks heading our way later it seemed the lady had discovered the truth, but she did return to speak to me after the ambassador's wife joined me for a chat. She was totally different, relaxed, no unnecessary airs and graces. She said she had been interested that a Scotsman was with an England football party and wondered not only why, but which part of Scotland I came from. She admitted later that she expected it to be Glasgow, Edinburgh or somewhere around that area.

When I said "Elgin," her eyes lit up.

"I was," she said, "educated in Nairn (some 20 miles from my hometown)."

From that point we had a thoroughly enjoyable reminiscing session – and a new view of me by the be-jewelled lady.

Next day it was back to business with the warm glow of that wonderful evening and a smile over the Embassy episode still present, and – Mexico v England, the main reason for our visit. The Azteca Stadium, where the game was staged, is a magnificent arena – and perhaps might have a lesson for some new grounds yet to be built.

Apparently the original plan had the whole place completely enclosed but the surface of the pitch didn't fare too well. So a huge barred gate was installed at each end and the stadium was able to 'breath'. Result; no more problems with the pitch.

The game? A fairly boring 0-0 draw, though it had one moment of high drama. Alan Mullery of Tottenham Hotspur and England was sent off and the crowd suddenly turned nasty. So much so that, away to the right of the Press box, a fight broke out on the terracing and two or three blood-spattered men were led away by the local police. Behind us, this caused another commotion with a man rising to his feet, firing a pistol into the air and shouting at the top of his voice.

After I'd straightened up – wouldn't you duck down if shots were being fired – I asked a local journalist what he had been saying? It appeared he had his two sons with him and no one was to come near him or them. No one did, understandably, though I saw a police officer edge into his company later.

Uraguay

From Mexico City it was off to URAGUAY, via CHILE and ARGENTINA. Simple eh? Well not quite. The plane was big and comfortable, the arrangement well made, but no one had reckoned on an electrical storm, a bad landing in Chile and an unpleasant stop over in Buenos Aires.

The storm struck as we were making our way down the east coast of South America. On our right we had lightning flashing and what I took to be St Elmo's fire rippling along the wings of our plane. On the left, in all their snow-tipped harsh beauty, were the sharp-toothed Andes mountains. If we had known that everything was to end peacefully it would have been all right, but while the storm was at its peak you couldn't help wondering.

Because I had been sleeping poorly I had been given a sleeping tablet, but it didn't work during the nervy journey – actually it cut in on the first day in Montevideo and I collapsed at my bed-side, awake but with my legs refusing to function. Fortunately the problem only lasted a couple of hours. The landing in Santiago, Chile, was an unusually bad one with our bouncing arrival throwing up clouds of red dust from a runway . . . well I think it was a runway, though what so much red dust was doing on site I don't know.

Finally, it was Buenos Aires and a short trip across the River Plate and the sight of the scuttled German battleships Schamhorst and Gneisenau to Montevideo and the welcome arrival at our hotel. Well, that is what we expected. In fact we were herded into several small rooms near Buenos Aires airport and, almost a day later, we were still there having had, in my case at least, only three small cups of thick black coffee and a couple of biscuits and a sleep on a chair.

Leading the protest was Alan Ball, the Blackpool, Everton, Arsenal and England player with the seeming ability to keep going long after others were completely exhausted. But even his angry outbursts left the Argentine officials completely unmoved as did the more diplomatic approaches by officials with the party.

When the impasse did come to an end, the promised planes big enough to take the party in two lots to our destination didn't materialise. I found myself in a small single-engine craft carrying four of us and flown by a pilot who didn't say a word other than those needed to take off and land.

Welcome to Uruguay. Over the many years of my life I have not heard of anyone who holidayed in Uruguay – and, though I haven't gone deeply into the subject, don't know of any holiday firms raving about tourist deals to go there. I was only in the place a few days and possibly misjudged it, but on that admittedly flimsy evidence I'm not surprised.

Montivideo was grey skies and rain for our whole stay and hard though the lady assigned to help the Press tried – she had a limp and walked with the aid of a stick, but seemed always to be on the move – the place was depressing.

It wasn't helped by a mistake a few of us made on the second night. I am still convinced we were told by the hotel reception to make a left turn out of the front door (they claimed they said "right turn") and we ended in a bar/restaurant reminiscent of those you see on films where the clientele all look rough and tough, the ladies (!!) of 'easy virtue' and the barman sleazy.

The food wasn't all that bad when it did come, but I had one drink, allegedly a small whisky, and almost immediately felt groggy. Fortunately I took it after food and was quickly hustled back to the hotel by my pals and into bed, where I slept solidly for about 12 hours which made it two solid sleeps in two nights, neither of them the kind which leaves you wakening fresh and raring to go. Oh! and England won 2-1 in a game which I didn't enjoy in a stadium that I didn't like. Sour grapes? Could be after the rain, the greyness and these two bad nights.

Rio de Janerio

Next stop was the boyhood dream – Rio! So often, when a lifelong dream becomes reality it is a disappointment. Not this time. Everything I expected of this great South American city became reality. The temperature was hot, hot, hot and humid, but I enjoyed it; the beaches, particularly Copacabana and Iponema were all that I expected and the imposing Sugar Loaf Mountain with the massive statue of Christ on the hilltop exactly as I had pictured them in my mind's eye.

Every morning – as was a habit of mine, and I later found, of Scottish football writer John Mann – I went for a jog on a beach whenever our work took us to seaside places. And jogging on a Rio beach has a problem – or maybe that should be a distraction . . . lots of bikini-clad (or even less) girls also jogging, or strolling and mostly laughing before heading for whatever work in which they were involved. I gamely managed to keep my concentration on the task I had set myself but it was difficult, very difficult.

Another aspect of my beach visits was seeing on several occasions lines of girls and groups of every skin colour possible, from blonde, white to deep black obviously enjoying each others company. It was surely a lesson to the rest of the world that whether you are black or white-skinned or any shade in between is of no real importance in the general scheme of things.

But back to football where I have never made any secret of the fact that I am an unashamed fan of Brazil and the way they play the game. It was on this visit that I learned why they keep producing players of a skill standard way beyond that of other countries.

Close to the beaches were areas of soft sand and on these, groups of young lads played games ranging from half-a-dozen-a-side to numbers which fluctuated from 20-plus upward and downward for no apparent reason. I don't know if you have ever tried to play football with a ball all the way up to full-size on a soft sand surface but I personally found it almost impossible. Not these boys. They ran about producing ball control and skills as if the surface was the perfectly manicured pitches like, Wembley or Hampden.

As I watched them one morning I was joined by Alan Ball and Brian Labone, both of Everton and England. After about ten minutes I suggested they join in a game. Alan, whom I never saw duck out of a challenge on the football field, looked at me as though I had suggested a swim with sharks.

"You are joking," he said "and I wouldn't want to spoil their fun anyway."

Brian just drifted away with a smile.

Rio was all I had expected – and still had a surprise for me. Their Football Association put on a meal for the England party including the Press. As I wandered round our table looking for my name I did a double take at one which I spotted at the next table. It was R. Rodriguez McGregor! The exclamation mark is mine – after all a Scot travelling with England in Brazil does not expect to find a local person with a Scottish-type name also present. I found out later that he was a Brazilian and when he took his place he certainly had nothing like a Scottish appearance.

When the meal was over I managed to get to him before he left and, though I didn't speak Portuguese and he had only a smattering of English, I did glean via bits and pieces that a grandfather, or great-grandfather had come from Scotland to help build bridges, though he hadn't known him. Which part of Scotland? Again nothing definite, but when I reeled off Glasgow, Edinburgh, Dundee, Perth, Aberdeen and Inverness the only reaction was to Inverness – 36 miles from where I was born.

I would dearly have loved to have had more time – and an interpreter – with us, but he had a business appointment and I had arranged a chat with a couple of players back at their hotel, so the full story remains a mystery and one which has niggled away at me since our meeting. After all I was a reporter and unfinished stories are a disappointment, to say the least.

As our time in Rio was rapidly running out and the game against Brazil was approaching, I had a notebook full of stories for my paper, *The Weekly News*. Now, many things make a reporter's life difficult and probably top of the heap is lack of communication with the place where their stories are recorded and printed. Today's lines of that communication are so complete that it is a bit of a sensation if they fail but this was before those days and, try as I might, I could not get on the telephone to any of our offices in Britain.

Fortunately before I left on the trip, a meeting in our Manchester office had established the fact that problems could arise and an amazing possible solution emerged. A member of our London staff had a friend who was an air hostess and she had friends who flew to Brazil as part of their job. In an emergency I was to contact an air hostess at her hotel in Rio and she would, with others along the way, get my copy to London. Because I didn't expect problems I noted the idea, but didn't have much faith in it.

Here I was with the crisis a fact. So it was off to the hotel – not far from the one I was staying in, and a meeting with an air hostess who knew exactly what had been arranged and was flying out in a few hours. So I relaxed? Not on your life. I still had to be convinced that she would hand my notes to someone else and they to a third party en route to London and that these notes would be collected by a member of our London staff when the final 'carrier' arrived.

But everything worked like a dream! My understanding afterwards was that the flights involved had been Rio-Tenerife; Tenerife-Paris and Paris-London and that the handovers had been perfectly executed. You will appreciate however, that I stayed pretty uptight until I had a copy of *The Weekly News* in my possession back home and saw the stories in print.

The game against Brazil? England lost 2-1, mostly because it was June, several players showed signs of fatigue in the closing stages and one of them, the excellent Keith Newton, of Blackburn Rovers and later Everton, lost concentration for a split second at left back. He let a ball he would normally have controlled with ease slip under his foot and, the opposition being Brazil, it was in the net almost before his foot was back on the ground.

From my point of view, though, I had at last been in my Stadium of Dreams, the world-famous Maracana. It could hold 250,000, the attendance that day was around 150,000 and, to be honest, it was looking a bit careworn. What did that matter to me? I was there where I had always wanted to be, I saw the inimitable Pele play on his home turf and Brazil dazzle in their own environment.

And before we leave, a bit of personal history. In the next Press box seat to me should have been Desmond Hackett.

Des's contrived bye-line as chief sports writer with the then massively circulating *Daily Express* was 'The man in the Brown Bowler.' Prior to Des it had been Henry Rose 'The Man in the Black Bowler' – and both did, in fact, wear the headgear when working.

The Hackett seat was empty when the game started but just before his phone started ringing. I waited, but no-one appeared, so I lifted and answered a request to "speak to Des" with, "sorry, he isn't here at the moment, but I'll tell him you've been on."

Around half-time it rang again, with a request for a report. I'd heard by this time that Des wasn't to be available because of 'a spot of tummy trouble.' I explained this and offered to put over some of my notes so that they could build a story of the first half. This was accepted. Near the end I repeated the offer and again it was accepted. I left it to the

Express people themselves to use the notes to build a story of the game and work out an introduction, which they did.

On a later trip with England to the Continent, Des thanked me for what I had done and, next morning, there was a bottle of champagne at the door of my hotel room – from him, though he never said so.

Rivalry in journalism is fierce, but there is friendship too and we had always got on well together. As a post-script to what was a wonderful experience – overall. We had a stop-over in Tenerife on the way back to Britain and I had the pleasure (?) of a fellow journalist, who was noted for his pessimism, telling me that, as we flew into the island, we could be on exactly the same flight path as a plane which had crashed killing everyone not long before. A frightening electric storm on the way down the Andes, Uruguay, now this information . . . as I say, OVERALL it was a wonderful experience.

Los Angeles

It was seventeen years on from Rio that I made it to my other 'dream city', LOS ANGELES. After Rio, LA disappointed me and had friends of our friend Dorothy Hampsey, from Manchester, not been wonderful hosts and given Alistair MacDonald of the *Aberdeen Press and Journal* and myself a tour of the city, I would have been more disappointed.

Among the sights, we saw the Hollywood sign (with one of the letter 'L' missing) relatively close up, the homes of many movie stars, including that of one of my particular favourites James Stewart, and, in the beach area, the muscle men strutting their stuff and the very lightly clad female roller-skaters gliding about seemingly effortlessly.

It was Scotland heading for World Cup duty in 1986 which took me to America first. Charlie Nicholas, of Celtic and Arsenal – and later a television critic of the game – had been in Libya with Arsenal and at the time you might as well have thrown a bomb on to the Custom Officer's desk as mention the name of Colonel Gadaffi's country anywhere in America.

As Kevin Keegan had done years before in the then Yugoslavia, Charlie disappeared into a back room, hustled there a group of officious individuals. Unlike Keegan however, he was treated to a stream of questions rather than a beating, which didn't stop the rest of the party expressing displeasure at (a) the treatment being meted out to one of our number; and (b) the long, boring wait until he was cleared.

A nervy start indeed but, Charlie cleared of any dastardly plot, at last we headed off to SANTA FE. The pre-Mexico idea was that the players would first train at altitude (Santa Fe is 7199 feet above ground level, Ben Nevis, Britain's highest mountain, is 4408 feet) then move on to Los Angeles which is at sea level.

The idea is apparently the best way to juggle round the red and white blood corpuscles in an athlete's body so that he (or she) is perfectly prepared for their efforts at altitude – Mexico City, where the Scots were to be stationed is 8000 feet above sea level.

So Santa Fe it was first. Indian country for those of us weaned on Hollywood movies and also immortalised (?) in the song about the Atchison, Topeka and Santa Fe railway line. Being pretty fit although no athlete, I didn't think twice about the altitude business. After all, I wasn't going to be running about, doing exercises and kicking a ball.

So when I strolled downhill for my first evening meal I enjoyed the walk and the food (even though cannabis cigarettes were being openly smoked in the restaurant and in several other spots I visited).

Then I set off back up what had appeared a not-too-steep hill on the way down. Halfway my legs all but gave out. A strategic pause as if adjusting my shoe-laces gave me the wee break I was needing before I set off again. I made it back from there, did a small piece of writing then went to bed for a sound sleep, unusual for me in a new bed on the first night of any trip.

"Altitude or jet lag?" I asked the doctor next day.

"Maybe a bit of both," he opined, which meant he wasn't sure. Neither was I, but I was never bothered again – in Santa Fe or Mexico City.

We witnessed of the most amazing thunder and lightning storms I had ever seen, somewhere between Santa Fe and Albuquerque and had a great meeting with the Northern Ireland party, stationed in Albuquerque with that wonderful Everton winger Billy Bingham, now retired as a player, as manager. My winning a large lump of money on an indoor horse-racing game failed to make Santa Fe more than just a stop-off on the way to the World Cup, though I would have liked to explore it at leisure.

Could be Scotland centre half Richard Gough doesn't think back to the Irish meeting as fondly. In a bounce game Scotland-Ireland in Albuquerque, he took a nasty cut after a clash of heads and looked for a short time as if he would miss the big competition altogether. Fortunately he was a fast healer and made it.

And the money? I put it on the bar for drinks all round, was tipped off that the barman used a fair bit of it for himself to buy measures and mount a challenge to Scotch whisky, which he didn't usually drink, and didn't turn up next day. A bad move all round as I was reliably informed when I went to have a chat with him about using money that wasn't his that he then lost his job.

As I was advised when I was young, "Enjoy whisky, but always be its master – never let it master you." He wasn't and lost!

* * *

So next it was a return for me to LOS ANGELES, down in the sense that we were heading for sea level after our 'sky-high' stint. Read about LA the way visiting film stars and the like describe it and it is heaven on earth or at the centre of the universe. They are of course, biased – either going there on a lucrative contract or trying to get one. I was there with no axe to grind and for a different purpose.

The hotel we were living in was at the airport and I'll swear pilot's line up the room I occupied as their guiding line into the main runway. Not that I objected – keeping the curtains open and watching them head their planes seemingly straight for you was a change from getting my head down over my laptop computer and reeling off the daily stories for *The Courier* back in Dundee.

Yes, my laptop computer – a far cry from the frightening desktop monolith I had started typing on 40-plus years ago. The Imperial never broke down, mainly due to the attentions of a typewriter mechanic gainfully employed all over Elgin and beyond, keeping the infernal beasts up to scratch.

The laptop, on the other hand suffered from may ailments on a regular basis. It was heavier than the portable typewriter I had carried on assignments for many years needed charging regularly and was definitely less dependable. The first time I tried to use it in Los Angeles nothing happened and while you could always get a typewriter working again because it was, basically, a simple instrument, the electronics of the laptop were beyond most of those who used it in those early days. With only minimal knowledge of how the thing worked I tried to resurrect it, but to no avail.

What to do with weeks of regular writing and sending back the articles to head office in Dundee ahead of me? The only answer was to telephone head office and make contact with the technical top man on laptops, John Allan. He responded magnificently and worked me through a series of key-tapping which finally saw life return to the seemingly dead machine. It took an hour on the telephone, but probably saved a huge sum of money as, had it not been revived, I would have been returning to the old-fashioned method of telephoning column after column of stories at huge cost, whereas the laptop zipped then over in a very small fraction of the time.

It very nearly let me down one more time. Los Angeles is described as the world centre of technology, but half way through sending my copy one night – I had to attach two rubber-lined earpieces to the telephone to do this – the strange screeching noise which told me everything was working suddenly stopped.

Panic! Try as I might I couldn't get back the connection, so I called the hotel reception and was calmly told by the operator that there had been a problem at one of the telephone companies and computers all over the place were being affected. If I was patient, I was assured, everything would be OK. Now patience in those circumstances is not easy to achieve, but I managed and sure enough, I got back in touch shortly after. LA the world centre of technology? Not for me while I was there!

Mexico City

And so it was on to Mexico City for the object of the whole exercise, the World Cup, which Scotland has got badly out of the habit of qualifying for, but which, was, around this time, a regular occurrence.

Jock Stein, the man who made Celtic the first British team ever to win the European Cup with his home-grown squad in 1967 – they were all Scottish, hailing from in and around Glasgow – had been in charge during the qualifying rounds. Sadly, he died of a heart attack while in the dug-out watching Scotland-Wales during that campaign. Alex Ferguson, the successful manager of Aberdeen was brought in to take charge.

None of us knew then what was ahead of the Govan-born, former none too successful centre-forward with Rangers, among other clubs; manager of Manchester United, trophies galore, including the European Cup even a knighthood and a claim that he was the best British manager of all time. In England, and even before, he had a reputation for not exactly being at ease with the media.

The chip-on-the-shoulder mentality which developed in later years was partly caused by the way he was treated by the English media in his early days, as he strove to get Manchester United back to greatness and struggled for results as a consequence. He doesn't forget slights, as many journalists were to find out.

In America and Mexico, however, he was co-operative with the media and relaxed whenever we had dealings with him, which was almost daily. Perhaps it was because he knew he was only there briefly and because of the death of a legendary figure; perhaps he felt at home amongst his countrymen and also almost certainly he knew managing Manchester United could be in the offing. A very private chat with United 'ambassador' Bobby Charlton during a training session was dismissed as 'a visit from an old friend – but was it?

Alex became United manager only months later, so whatever the reason everything went well – except, as usual, the results.

Chapter Eighteen

Another Scotland World Cup Failure

Anyone who has followed Scotland in recent years would not object to a 'reincarnation' of exactly the same squad of players.

Goalkeepers – Jim Leighton (Aberdeen), Alan Rough (Hibs), Andy Goram (Oldham Athletic); defence and midfield – Richard Gough, Marice Malpas, David Narey, Eamonn Bannon (all Dundee United), Graeme Souness (Sampdoria), Alex McLeish, Willie Miller, Jim Bett (Aberdeen), Roy Aitken, Paul McStay (Celtic), Steve Archibald (Barcelona), Graeme Sharp (Everton), Charlie Nicholas (Arsenal), Paul Sturrock (Dundee United), Davie Cooper (Rangers).

The five Dundee United players thoroughly deserved their places as did the key men in the most successful Aberdeen team. Archibald and Souness were plying their trade successfully in two of the greatest football countries in the world; every one of the others was a genuine star at the club level.

And that just might be the root cause of Scotland's failure again and again at World Cup level. Why the journey beyond the first round has always proved too much. Once they reach above the ordinary and into the rarefied atmosphere of the later rounds of the biggest tournament of all, the players retain their individual skills, which were good enough to get them to the finals, but as a team they don't add to that the essential blend of talents.

We Scots are noted as being individuals rather than team players in many walks of life. It leads to personal success, but so seldom, in sport at least, to team achievements. It has happened in football at club level rather than the international game – Jock Stein's Celtic are the prime example – but not above that where the country is being represented.

So we set off in Mexico with the usual belief that if we didn't win the World Cup we would get damned close – and ended with the usual failure even to qualify for the later rounds.

A close call against Denmark (lost 1-0); a wonderful opening goal by Gordon Strachan against the might of West Germany (but lost 2-1) and a 0-0 draw against Uruguay . . . this game deserving special mention for its violence.

I had just settled in my seat and turned to watch the game when midfielder Batista launched himself at Strachan and caught him about waist high with a tackle that could have sent the 'wee man' into intensive care. Less than a minute had been played and obviously the Uruguayans had marked the Manchester United star as the main danger to them after his goal against the Germans. And 'marked' is the appropriate word in the circumstances.

Fortunately Strachan suffered no permanent damage and rightly the referee took a decision – even that early – to send off the thug who had made the tackle (Note – to all referees. A dirty, dangerous tackle is as bad in the first minute of a game as the last and should be punished by sending off the perpetrator, as it was in this case).

So we were homeward bound after failure – yet again! To this day I wonder if the much younger Fergie made at least one decision which was wrong. He left Graeme Souness out of the Uruguay game. It was said that Souness was at the stage of his career where he wouldn't have lasted the game on full throttle. Maybe he wouldn't, but with his experience he could have exerted a tremendous influence on it while making sure that the Uruguayans were 'out-physicalled' when they chose that style of play!

The football, as they say done and dusted, Mexico, in this case Mexico City, left memories as the country had in my earlier excursion with England. Training was held on the edge of the city and as I stepped out of our plush hotel in the city centre and boarded the air conditioned luxury bus to attend the first session, I was fully aware of how lucky we were and how great a job I had.

This was hammered home when we stepped off the bus. Across from the football ground was a huge municipal rubbish dump – and on that dump were refuse lorries unloading their 'cargo' AND people scrabbling about around them! As the training was to go on for at least an hour – the players were still getting acclimatised to the heat – I knew I couldn't get any chats for quite a time, so I went over the road to the edge of the dump. Not only were people fighting for scraps from the lorry-loads, but there were also ramshackle buildings on the dump where, I confirmed, they actually lived.

Now when I think I am being hard done to, I recall that scene . . .

Mexico City is absolutely massive as I found out on my first visit, and the six lanes of traffic heading in each direction were still there, as nose-to-tail as ever. There had been a disastrous earthquake a year or so before and on street corners traders were busy at stalls selling off bits and pieces they had retrieved from the wreckage.

Heartless? One man's explanation to me (in a flawless American accent) was, "The owners died, no one claimed them (he had a selection of rings) so what's wrong with us finding them and selling them?"

I suggested, probably naively, that an attempt to find relatives of the owners might have been a good idea and he suddenly couldn't speak English any more, just his native tongue, which didn't sound Mexican-Spanish to me.

That night, I woke to find the hotel shaking. Before I could get out of bed to find out what was going on it stopped. I waited, nothing more happened, so I phoned the desk.

"Only a slight after-shock," I was told by a man who sounded as though he was surprised that I was asking.

I had no experience of earthquakes, but a great long-distance respect for them. For a few seconds, which seemed like hours, my appreciation of the fear they could cause when at full blast grew enormously.

And as a post-script to my second Mexico 'adventure,' a story of a strange meeting and a worrying departure.

First, the meeting. I was standing in front of a fence at the Scotland training ground watching the players being put through their paces when a voice from the other side of the fence piped up, "any body frae the Dundee Courier here?" Now it wasn't unusual for people, wherever you were in the world, to ask to speak to someone from a newspaper, usually one they read or had read back home, but I had never been approached this way before.

As I answered "yes," I turned, to find a dark-haired, heavily sun-tanned man in what looked about his mid-thirties and lightly dressed in shirt, white shorts and scruffy sandal-type footwear moving to be opposite me on the other side of the fence.

"How's Dundee?" he asked in a still well defined Dundee accent.

"Fine," I replied cautiously. Then he launched into a succession of questions about landmarks and pubs in the city. When he paused, I asked why his interest, what was his connection with Dundee? As a reporter I saw a nice personal story coming.

His answer, a suddenly very unfriendly, "None of your f.....g business" and off he trotted.

With the fence between us and the nearest gate a long way away and in the opposite direction to which he was headed, I could only watch him disappear and to this day wonder who he was and why he didn't want publicity.

The start of our visit, the American questioning of Charlie Nicholas, hadn't been fun and neither was our departure. As we lined up to leave at the airport, I suddenly realised I had lost a vital yellow slip of paper which had to be handed over before we could board our plane. Behind the desk was a man with more medal ribbons on his jacket than I have ever seen on any individual before or since – and as he was also fat, the jacket stretched over a considerable area.

The fact I was with the Scotland party and that I had every other piece of paper required made not the slightest difference. It was "produce the yellow slip or else!" After about ten minutes of argument, I took a breather to work out my next move. And it was obvious. As if giving in I went to the desk, said sorry for the bother I was causing and turned away, then back. Next to the man refusing my requests was a younger lad who seemed to have a good grasp of English. I asked him if, before we resumed negotiations, I could have a history of some of the medals his boss was wearing (by this time everyone except Martin Frizell of the *News of the World* – having a similar problem to me – had moved on).

The request was passed on and using the younger man as an interpreter, though I am sure he didn't need him, I was informed of the history of the top layer and several below that. Then suddenly he stopped talking, paused and grunted out a command. A paper was passed in front of me for signing – I think Martin was also presented with one – and after we had done that we were told we were free to join the rest of the party.

Though I wanted to do something else, which would probably have ended with me doing a few years in a Mexican prison, I shook the medallion man's hand and was greeted with what might be described as a smile of triumph at holding me up and of pleasure that I recognised how important he was?

I didn't know – and certainly wasn't going to hang about to analyse the answer.

Chapter Nineteen

Italy 1990 . . .
and Yet Another Failure

The years were rolling on, 48 behind me as a reporter, only two ahead when I covered my last and fourth (three with Scotland, one with England) World Cup tournament.

This was in Italy in 1990 and it proved the least enjoyable of the lot.

Scotland was now managed by Andy Roxburgh, whose knowledge of the technicalities of the game was unrivalled. However, for my money, he didn't have the ability to get this knowledge over to players. Scotland had qualified for the world's biggest football tournament for an amazing fifth time in succession. Amazing when you consider how seldom qualification has happened since and how much we over-rate ourselves. There was a time when we were indeed up there with the top nations, but that was long, long ago now and we have slipped and are slipping further and further behind.

Right from the start of the usual few weeks in Italy before we were eliminated I had the feeling that the players listened to what Roxburgh had to say, but didn't take in most of it. There had been tremendous respect for Jock Stein, something similar for Alex Ferguson, because of his burgeoning reputation with Aberdeen but Andy didn't seem to impress the same way.

As always, the 'ammunition' was there for Scotland to make a real impression in the tournament, as always things didn't work out that way. It wasn't for lack of experience – eight of the playing party had been in the World Cup squad of four years before – Jim Leighton, Alex McLeish, Roy Aitken, Richard Gough, Paul McStay, Maurice Malpas, Jim Bett and Andy Goram. The new lads included midfielders Steward McCall, John Collins and Gary McAllister, and strikers Gordon Durie and Ally McCoist, all of whom went on to build great reputations in the game at club level. Out of that batch alone you would imagine a team could be formed capable of doing a good job.

Yet again, this wasn't the case. When you looked at Group C, where Scotland were drawn, it wasn't difficult to imagine four points gathered – which actually turned out to be the qualifying total – from Brazil, Sweden and Costa Rica.

Certainly Costa Rica, qualifying for the very first time in their existence and completely new to such a big stage, should have been two points in the bag. But the very fact that 'certainties' had come unstuck so often before should have warned us of the dangers of over-optimism. And, sure enough, the newcomers threw the usual spanner in the Scotland works.

In Genoa on June 11, they won 1-0.

It could be said we weren't the only ones to underestimate them as they defeated Sweden, again in Genoa, 2-1 nine days later and qualified from the Section along, inevitably, with Brazil. Scotland rallied against Sweden in Genoa and won 2-1, but, unsurprisingly, lost 1-0 to Brazil in Turin in the final game. Result – three games, two points, a two for, three against goal difference and the usual early exit from the tournament.

Reputations were partly salvaged in the Brazil game, where it took the wonderfully talented South Americans until nine minutes from the end to get their winning goal via Mueller, but the whole exercise was yet another failure.

Italy is a wonderful place to visit, the food, the weather and just about everything else is perfect, but you will excuse me if I didn't appreciate the pluses fully with the minus of yet again seeing my country's football team promise so much and achieve so little. It didn't help a lot, either that there was the usual pompous rubbish from Scottish Football Association officials.

One club director, who was noted for his attendance at every function where there was free food and drink and who travelled the world on the money put into the game by genuine supporters, met myself and a colleague after one Press conference with the words, "Free-loading as usual . . . what a wonderful life you Press lot have."

I was used to this sort of stupidity so merely listed the free meals he'd had since leaving home, the cost of his hotel room and one or two 'incidentals' before he was pulled away by a more sober colleague, who at least had the common sense to say "Sorry, he's had a few."

Then there was SFA secretary Jim Farry. As one of half-a-dozen football writers who turned up at the team's hotel after a training session, I was astonished to find the portly Mr Ferry at the main entrance telling us we had to use "The tradesman's entrance round the back," adding that the players weren't giving interviews.

Without hesitation I pointed out that I always used the main entrance to a hotel and was about to do it again and that if he tried to stop me he would regret it. As I was backed unanimously by my colleagues, he had the sense to step aside.

First person I saw when I went inside was Richard Gough. Richard had lived two doors along from me in Dundee when he played for United. (his then manager Jim McLean told me on one occasion that he was sure it was me who was trying to get Richard a transfer. This was totally untrue, although we did talk football when we met and he did move to Tottenham Hotspur, then Rangers later).

But back to Italy.

"No interviews today?" I said.

"Who told you that?" was the Gough answer.

"Jim Farry," I replied.

"He's talking rubbish, what do you want to know," Richard replied, plonking himself on a comfortable sofa where I joined him before asking questions. I hadn't even thought of them before arriving because I hadn't expected the stupidity we met at the main entrance.

As a sidelight to the Italian (mis)adventure, it is interesting to note that Roxburgh, in 1994, moved on to become technical director of UEFA and has just retired from the post. This I feel, was his real strength – the statistics, the facts, the projections about football – not managing a bunch of footballers of mixed ability, temperament and application.

The early 1980's had been golden years for the 'New Firm' of Dundee United and Aberdeen and I'd been with United all over Europe, but as the 1990s came in their stock was descending and the old Celt-Rangers monopoly was taking hold again in Scotland. I still loved my football and enjoyed watching Forfar Athletic, for instance – an excellent side around this time – as much as more famous teams.

I was at the stage of life where you are inclined to look back and wonder where the years went. When I did just that I had few, very few, regrets in my personal or working life. As someone summed up on my retiral day,

"You've seen it all, done it all and got the proverbial T-shirt. Good time to go."

Not very original, but certainly accurate from that nervous beginning in Elgin so long ago through countless events to 130 miles away in Dundee. In between, a huge heap of stories, an uncountable number of miles travelled, an amazing number of people interviewed . . . and that most important thing of all when you talk about work – job satisfaction.

Retiral

I had the most wonderful send-off – lunch with colleagues I'd known for years and enjoyed working with, then a party organised by my wife and kept secret where family and more friends, many from the world of football and totalling about 80 from all over Britain – wined, snacked and danced the night away. I just remember getting a taxi home, but will never forget that party!

So for the first time since I was 14 I was out of work. To some that is a wonderful feeling, to others a nightmare. I have one friend who was so scared of his pending retiral that he confessed to me the reason.

"How are me and her (his wife) going to live together every hour of every day of what's left of our lives," he agonised.

I had no such problem, though you never assume too much in life. Mildred and I live happily, with the only regret that, work circumstances having divided the family, we don't see as much of our children, grand-children and now, great grand-children as we might.

Chapter Twenty

Full Time

Now as I sit having a cuppa or a coffee in our bungalow in Fife my mind is inclined to wander back to incidents, sparked in the memory by a comment, a news item in a paper, on the radio or television from my 50 years as a reporter.

Seeing David Burnside, then of Wolves, giving an exhibition of football skills which defied belief at half-time in a game at Ibrox Park in Glasgow, and realising that ball skills alone may entertain, but don't necessarily make a top level player.

Most players can play tricks with a football, but they best use these tricks only when it gives them an advantage in a competitive game. They have skills more important within a team – among them linking with their team mates, passing accurately, taking scoring chances if they are forwards, preventing scoring chances if they are defenders. Being fit enough to last not 90 minutes, but 120 and beyond – as the janitor at my first school, East End, Elgin, small, balding but curly haired Sandy Robertson used to say when training us for athletics, "Don't aim to just break the tape, go flat out for at least ten yards beyond it".

His accurate theory was that, if you aimed for the tape in any walk of life, you would probably slow down, a fraction before breaking it and lose out. Working to his formula I won three athletic championships and used it theoretically in most aspects of my life.

Arriving at as hotel in Yugoslavia and being handed, by a very attractive young woman, a list – of the sexual services available on each floor of the hotel. A purely technical study, without in any way getting involved, revealed that the higher the floor the more advanced (?) the offers. Which reminds me of a visit to Prague and a journalist availing himself of the opportunity for some physical relaxation. Returning from a meal elsewhere a few of us were met with the view of him, dishevelled looking, leaving a room shouting "Je suis normal" just ahead of a lady clad in black leather and carrying – yes – a whip. A definite case of bad choice!

Getting behind the counter of a Post Office in Guadalajara, Mexico and Sofia, Belgrade.

In both cases I had copy to send back to my office in Manchester and in both cases I was being completely ignored. So there was only one thing to do – and I did it.

Guadalajara proved the most risky as a guard, complete with drawn revolver rushed in from somewhere and confronted me. Amazingly, after a sort of stunned silence, the totally Mexican-speaking staff suddenly produced several people who spoke English, my situation was accepted and my copy duly dispatched while I was given a cup of coffee.

The difference in Sofia was that I was almost immediately grabbed by a matronly lady who said something to staff members who were obviously alarmed at this stranger arriving on their side of the counter. I was given a chair while they returned to their posts. We managed a sort of conversation between us and she went to a teleprinter and sent my stories to their destination; though hers being the Cyrillic alphabet I was informed on my return that it had read, 'A bit weird.'

Struggling with a laptop computer, a new-fangled gadget to me, on a plane in the mid-eighties and having an obviously panic-stricken stewardess rushing me up and telling me, "You can't use that thing here, it could cause us to crash." Apparently the computer had in it electronic gizmos which could interfere with the navigation system on an aircraft and cause it to crash. I carefully switched off, put it back in its carrying case and got out the old-fashioned, but dependable, pen and paper.

Having a well-built lad approach me when I was visiting Aston Villa, while in England and lead with "You a Scottish reporter?" in a pronounced English accent. When I said "yes" he went on;

"I can play for Scotland, y'know, my father is Scottish though I was born in Aldershot."

I'd seen him play – he was a wing-half and a good one, so I did what I did in quite a number of cases, sent a note of his name and other details to Ernie Walker, then assistant secretary of the S.F.A., later secretary. The player's name was Bruce Rioch, he did play for Scotland – 24 times in all between 1975 and 1978 - and actually captained his 'adopted' country.

Trying to use my already booked phone in Rumania to report on Dundee United European Game. It was during the reign of the notorious dictator Nicolae Ceausescu and I was told by what I can only describe as a thug in a dark suit to leave all phoning to the young woman sitting beside it in the row in front of myself and other journalists. When I handed over the first of my typed match reports I spoke a few words to her and will never forget the terrified look on her face and her comment, "please do not speak to me or I will be punished" In her interests I didn't, while at the same time wondering how people in the modern day could be treated like this. That , however, wasn't all to dislike about the Rumania of those days. Wallace Moore of the *Daily Record* and me were still sending 'copy' when the Dundee United bus left for the airport and the return flight. We spoke to a local journalist who must have been either a brave man or someone with influence because he organized transport for us. It was a big black beast of a car and to get to it we were escorted by another dark-suited, non speaking, tough-looking young man through two gates –which had to be opened, then closed when we got through them – before getting into the car. It was then driven by yet another dark-suited, etc., who yet again didn't speak at all through the two gates, opened and then shut, to the airport. We made the flight in time – just! I certainly wouldn't have wanted to spend any more time there than necessary.

Going through Checkpoint Charlie to East Berlin in the Cold War Days. No bother at all going East, pleasant guards, sharing of cigarettes, chat with an English – speaking one about football. Easy. The main thing about our brief stroll on 'the other side' was the eeriness of empty streets, the absence of people. We saw, at most, three or four . . . plus one who followed us every inch of the way on the opposite side of the road! Then it was back to Checkpoint Charlie – and the feeling we were now classed as spies. First we were 'frisked' by the same guards as we had shared cigarettes with. They had worn holstered pistols earlier, now the holsters were open. Then "Where are your passports?" I replied "There" pointing at the drawer they had been put in. It was empty. Half an hour of this cat-and-mouse scenario went on until, suddenly, a guard came from somewhere to report that our passports had been found and handed them over. Gritting our teeth we thanked them (!) and walked back to the West . . . quickly.

The songs . . . I must have heard thousands as I travelled up and down Britain covering football, some so obscene that those singing them must be candidates for a mental home, some just plain stupid, some, especially at games in Glasgow and Northern Ireland, allegedly religious, but in reality full of bitterness and hatred – and some unforgettable.

Into the latter category come two in particular.

To this day I get a lump in the throat when I hear *You'll Never Walk Alone*. Dozens of singers have recorded it and they make a good fist of it at Celtic Park but I only hear it the way Gerry Marsden sang it and transferred it to the Kop and the other three sides of a packed Liverpool's Anfield 40 years ago and more. As it burrows its way into my mind, I see Bill Shankly, Bob Paisley, Joe Fagan, Ronnie Moran and the other original 'architects' of Liverpool FC's resurgence and entry into the top flight of club football standing proud as the red shirted Ron Yeats, Ian St John, Gordon Milne, Billy Stevenson, Roger Hunt, Ian Callaghan and the rest raced out from under the sign 'This Is Anfield' and on to the pitch.

Many of these men – and the original 'choir' – are no longer with us, but they and the song will always be with me.

I was equally a fan of the songs at another ground. I covered many Wales home games against Scotland and England at Ninian Park in Cardiff. Normally I was present 90 minutes before kick-off at any ground. Here it was two hours before, to get my chats with football folk, but more so to hear the singing. Whether or not it was deliberate I don't know, but the terracing to my right as I sat in the Press box would fill with what seemed to be massed male voice choirs long before kick-off. They would give non-stop renderings of classic Welsh 'anthems' up to kick-off and at half-time. Again that wonderful singing will always be with me, even though Ninian Park is mostly for memories of the past.

And how can a Scot of my vintage ever forget the songs and noise at Hampden Park, particularly when Scotland played England? I am talking about the real Hampden, not the little 50,000 ground it has become – better looking maybe, but a toy by comparison.

When 138,000 was the capacity and it was full, woe betide any reporter trying to phone his office. Even with the angled windows all shut, the noise of the singing made conversation impossible. It was a case of shouting down the line and hoping that the phone girls at the other end got what you were saying.

Ah, yes . . . football isn't all about football.

* * *

. . . And finally . . .

The most asked question of any football writer, especially when he (or she) retires is – what would be your best team from all the players you have seen?

The answer? Impossible because there have been so many, but I'll give a selection, sticking strictly to players born in Scotland, England, Wales and Ireland. I watched literally thousands in action over the period 1942-92, some great, some excellent, some good and some out of their depth at the top level.

Then there is the question of 2-3-5, 4-2-4, 4-3-3, 3-5-2, 4-5-1 and all the other weird concoctions coaches keep coming up with today.

I won't attempt to stay within those parameters, just give you the best players, as I see it, in goal, at full back, in central defence, in midfield at inside forward and up front . . . (some played with other teams but I will name them in the teams with which they are most likely to be associated). There is no order of preference, but from this group could emerge many super XI's, any of which I would be happy to pit against any opposition any time anywhere in the world.

GOAL – Jimmy Cowan of Morton is an almost forgotten figure, but, as a youngster he was a sensational arrival on the international scene and won 25 caps for Scotland between 1948 and 1952. He was also the first keeper to draw a line from penalty spot to goal-line "so that I could work out shooting angles" – a practice barred later by officialdom.

Bill Brown of Dundee and Tottenham Hotspur – his nickname, 'The Cat' says just about it all. And, from England, the great rivals, Gordon Banks and Peter Shilton, both of whom started with Leicester City.

FULL BACK – Alex Hamilton (Dundee), Danny McGrain, (Celtic), Eric Caldow (Rangers), Roger Byrne (Manchester United), sadly a victim of the Munich air disaster; Jimmy Armfield (Blackpool); Ray Wilson (Everton), Terry Cooper (Leeds United).

CENTRAL DEFENCE – George Young (Glasgow Rangers), Jack Vernon (Belfast Celtic,), Terry Butcher (Ipswich Town), John Charles (Leeds United) who was so good all-round that I will also name him among the strikers; Billy McNeil (Celtic), Richard Gough (Dundee United, Rangers).

MIDFIELD – Duncan Edwards (Manchester United again a victim of the Munich air disaster and so good all-round that he, like Charles, could play in almost any position; Dave Mackay (Hearts, Tottenham Hotspur, Derby County), Bobby Moore (West Ham United), Doug Cowie (Dundee), Dave Narey (Dundee United), Graeme Souness (Liverpool), Billy Bremner (Leeds United), Jim Baxter (Rangers), Bryan Robson (Manchester United).

INSIDE FORWARD – Billy Steel (Derby County and Dundee), Wilf Mannion (Middlesbrough), Raich Carter (Derby County), Peter Doherty (Derby County), Ernie Taylor (Blackpool), Bobby Johnstone (Hibs and Manchester City), Johnny Haynes (Fulham), Colin

Bell (Manchester City), Johnny Giles (Leeds United), John White (Tottenham Hotspur), Bobby Collins (Leeds United).

FORWARDS – George Best (Manchester United), Tom Finney (Preston North End), Jimmy Johnstone (Celtic), Willie Henderson (Rangers), Stanley Matthews (Stoke City and Blackpool), Bobby Charlton (Manchester United), Denis Law (Manchester United), Alan Gilzean (Dundee and Tottenham Hotspur), Tommy Lawton (Everton), Tommy Taylor (Manchester United) another Munich victim, Alex Young (Everton), Jimmy Greaves (Tottenham Hotspur), Ian Rush (Liverpool), John Charles (Leeds United), Davie Cooper (Rangers).

Only around 50 from thousands and I can predict now that people reading the list, while they might not disagree with most players named will prefer to berate me for the mistakes I have made in leaving out their particular favourites!

When you know these players as I did and appreciate their skills it could be argued that once you had picked the eleven for the day and a few substitutes, you could leave them to go out on the field and win a game, no matter the opposition. But, though they were true 'greats' of their era, they were not all by any means self-disciplined – think Best, Baxter and Steel as examples – so a manager who could control players, and get the best out of them by earning their respect would be necessary.

I cannot separate two though they could be challenged by at least half-a-dozen others – Sir Alf Ramsey and Sir Alex Ferguson, one immortalised at club and international level, the other at club level.

. . . and now I'll get into really deep waters – first by naming a Scotland team from 'my' era, then an England team, both in 2-3-5 formation (which doesn't really mean anything because of the quality of the players, who could adapt to any system).

Scotland – Cowan (Morton), McGrain (Celtic), Caldow (Rangers), Mackay (Spurs), Young (Rangers), Cowie (Dundee), Johnstone

(Celtic), Law (Manchester United), Gilzean (Spurs), Steel (Dundee), Cooper (Rangers). Team Captain – Young.

England – Banks (Stoke City), Byrne (Manchester United), Wilson (Everton), Edwards (Manchester United), Butcher (Ipswich Town), Moore (West Ham), Matthews (Stoke City), Bell (Manchester City), Lawton (Everton), Mannion (Middlesbrough), Finney (Preston North End). Captain – Moore.

So now I come to the end of my story of a working life where I had that wonderful privilege of job satisfaction with, of all things, an apology . . . to friends Bob and Bill Shankly, Bob Paisley, Sir Matt Busby, Don Revie, Joe Mercer, Bill Nicholson et al . . . yes, you would probably do just as good a job in charge lads, but like I said to you so often over the years when you criticised something I had written – "Fair enough, but that is my opinion and I stick by it."

Thank you and for all its faults, dear reader, enjoy the game as I have done from childhood to old age. It may be different in many, many ways from the one I fell in love with as a teenager, but the basic facts remain . . . a ball, 22 players on the field, a referee and two linesmen – OK assistant referees or something like that – biased supporters of both teams keeping the noise level high, reporters from newspapers expressing their opinion in print afterwards, trying to be fair and finding the age old criticism being levelled.

"WERE YOU AT THE SAME GAME?"

So different yet so much the same.